AT&T

VOLUME 3

SYSTEM ADMINISTRATION FACILITIES

UNIX*
programmer's manual

CBS COLLEGE PUBLISHING'S
UNIX SYSTEM LIBRARY

---

* Trademark of AT&T.

AT&T

VOLUME 3

SYSTEM ADMINISTRATION FACILITIES

UNIX*
programmer's manual

CBS COLLEGE PUBLISHING'S
UNIX SYSTEM LIBRARY

Steven V. Earhart: Editor

HOLT, RINEHART AND WINSTON
New York Chicago San Francisco Philadelphia
Montreal Toronto London Sydney Tokyo
Mexico City Rio de Janeiro Madrid

---

* Trademark of AT&T.

IMPORTANT NOTE TO USERS

This document was set on an AUTOLOGIC, Inc. APS-5 phototypesetter driven by the TROFF formatter operating under the UNIX system on an AT&T 3B20 computer.

---

* Trademark of AT&T.

Library of Congress Cataloging-in-Publication Data

UNIX programmer's manual.

  At head of title: AT&T
  Includes index.
  Contents: v. 1. Commands and utilities — v. 2.
System calls and library routines — v. 3. System
administration facilities.
  1. UNIX (Computer operating system)   I. Earhart,
Steven V.   II. American Telephone and Telegraph Company.
QA76.76.063U548   1986   005.4'3   86-311
Select Code   320-033
ISBN 0-03-009313-9

Printed in the United States of America

Published simultaneously in Canada

678   090   98765432

CBS COLLEGE PUBLISHING
Holt, Rinehart and Winston
The Dryden Press
Saunders College Publishing

PREFACE

The *UNIX Programmer's Manual* describes most of features of UNIX System V. It does not provide a general overview of the UNIX system nor details of the implementation of the system.

Not all commands, features, or facilities described in this series are available in every UNIX system implementation. For specific questions on a machine implementation of the UNIX system, consult your system administrator.

The *UNIX Programmer's Manual* is available in several volumes. The first three volumes consist of the following:

- Volume 1 contains the Commands and Utilities (sections 1 and 6).

- Volume 2 contains the System Calls and Library Routines (sections 2, 3, 4, and 5).

- Volume 3 contains the System Administration Facilities (sections 1M, 7, and 8).

TRADEMARKS

INTRODUCTION

The *UNIX Programmer's Manual — Volume 3: System Administration Facilities* is divided into three sections:

1M—System Administration Commands and Applications Programs

7—Special Files

8—System Maintenance Procedures

Section 1M (*System Administration Commands and Applications Programs*) contains system maintenance programs, such as *fsck*(1M), *crash*(1M), etc., which generally reside in the directory **etc**. These entries contain a sub-class designation of "1M" for cross-referencing reasons.

Section 7 (Special Files) discusses the characteristics of each system file that actually refers to an input/output device. Only files in general use are covered and this section should not be considered complete.

Section 8 (*System Maintenance Procedures*) discusses facility descriptions, remote job entry, etc.

Each section consists of a number of independent entries of a page or so each. The name of the entry appears in the upper corners of its page(s). Entries within each section are alphabetized, with the exception of the introductory entry that begins each section. Some entries may describe several routines, commands, etc. In such cases, the entry appears only once, under its "major" name.

All entries use a common format, not all of whose parts always appear:

> The **NAME** part gives the name(s) of the entry and briefly states its purpose.

> The **SYNOPSIS** part summarizes the use of the program described. A few conventions are used:

> **Boldface** strings are literals and are typed just as they appear.

Italic strings usually represent substitutable argument prototypes and program names found elsewhere in the *UNIX Programmer's Manual*.

Square brackets [ ] around an argument prototype indicate that the argument is optional. When an argument prototype is given as "name" or "file", it always refers to a *file* name.

Ellipses ... are used to show that the previous argument prototype may be repeated.

A final convention is used by the commands themselves. An argument beginning with minus −, plus +, or equal sign = is often taken to be a flag argument, even if it appears in a position where a file name could appear. Files that begin with −, +, or = should therefore be avoided.

The **DESCRIPTION** part discusses the subject.

The **EXAMPLE(S)** part provides example(s) of usage.

The **FILES** part shows the file names that are built into the program.

The **DIAGNOSTICS** part discusses the diagnostic indications that may be produced. Messages that are self-explanatory are not listed.

The **BUGS** section describes known deficiencies that exist on some implementations.

The **SEE ALSO** section suggests related utilities or information to consult.

The **WARNINGS** part describes potential pitfalls.

A table of contents and a permuted index precede Section 1M. The table of contents lists each major entry with a brief description and the page number that the entry begins on. The permuted index is used by searching the middle column for a key word or phrase. The right column contains the name of the utility along with the section number. The left column of the permuted index contains additional useful information about the utility or command.

Throughout this volume references to sections 2, 3, 4, and 5 can be found in the *UNIX Programmer's Manual—Volume 2: System Calls and Library Routines*. References to sections 1 and 6 will be found in the *UNIX Programmer's Manual—Volume 1: Commands and Utilities*.

TABLE OF CONTENTS

1M. System Administration Commands and Applications Programs

7. Special Files

8. System Maintenance Procedures

PERMUTED INDEX

NAME

intro — introduction to system maintenance commands and application programs

DESCRIPTION

This section describes, in alphabetical order, commands that are used chiefly for system maintenance and administration purposes. The commands in this section should be used along with those listed in Sections 1 and 6 of the *UNIX Programmer's Manual — Volume 1: Commands and Utilities* and Sections 2, 3, 4, and 5 of the *UNIX Programmer's Manual — Volume 2: System Calls and Library Routines*. References to other manual entries not of the form *name*(1M), *name*(7) or *name*(8) refer to entries of the above volumes.

COMMAND SYNTAX

Unless otherwise noted, commands described in this section accept options and other arguments according to the following syntax:

name [*option*(*s*)] [*cmdarg*(*s*)]
where:

name	The name of an executable file.
option	— *noargletter*(*s*) or, — *argletter*<>*optarg* where <> is optional white space.
noargletter	A single letter representing an option without an argument.
argletter	A single letter representing an option requiring an argument.
optarg	Argument (character string) satisfying preceding *argletter*.
cmdarg	Path name (or other command argument) *not* beginning with — or, — by itself indicating the standard input.

SEE ALSO

getopt(1) in the *UNIX Programmer's Manual—Volume 1: Commands and Utilities.*

getopt(3C) in the *UNIX Programmer's Manual—Volume 2: System Calls and Library Routines.*

DIAGNOSTICS

Upon termination, each command returns two bytes of status, one supplied by the system and giving the cause for termination, and (in the case of "normal" termination) one supplied by the program (see *wait* (2) and *exit* (2)). The former byte is 0 for normal termination; the latter is customarily 0 for successful execution and non-zero to indicate troubles such as erroneous parameters, bad or inaccessible data, or other inability to cope with the task at hand. It is called variously "exit code", "exit status", or "return code", and is described only where special conventions are involved.

BUGS

Regretfully, many commands do not adhere to the aforementioned syntax.

NAME

accept, reject — allow/prevent LP requests

SYNOPSIS

/usr/lib/accept destinations
/usr/lib/reject [−r[reason]] destinations

DESCRIPTION

Accept allows *lp*(1) to accept requests for the named *destinations*. A *destination* can be either a printer or a class of printers. Use *lpstat*(1) to find the status of *destinations*.

Reject prevents *lp*(1) from accepting requests for the named *destinations*. A *destination* can be either a printer or a class of printers. Use *lpstat*(1) to find the status of *destinations*. The following option is useful with *reject*.

−r[*reason*]   Associates a *reason* with preventing *lp* from accepting requests. This *reason* applies to all printers mentioned up to the next −r option. *Reason* is reported by *lp* when users direct requests to the named *destinations* and by *lpstat*(1). If the −r option is not present or the −r option is given without a *reason*, then a default *reason* will be used.

FILES

/usr/spool/lp/*

SEE ALSO

lpadmin(1M), lpsched(1M).
enable(1), lp(1), lpstat(1) in the *UNIX Programmer's Manual — Volume 1: Commands and Utilities.*

NAME
     acctdisk, acctdusg, accton, acctwtmp — overview of accounting and
     miscellaneous accounting commands

SYNOPSIS
     /usr/lib/acct/acctdisk

     /usr/lib/acct/acctdusg [**—u** file] [**—p** file]

     /usr/lib/acct/accton [file]

     /usr/lib/acct/acctwtmp "reason"

DESCRIPTION
     Accounting software is structured as a set of tools (consisting of
     both C programs and shell procedures) that can be used to build
     accounting systems. *Acctsh*(1M) describes the set of shell pro-
     cedures built on top of the C programs.

     Connect time accounting is handled by various programs that write
     records into **/etc/utmp**, as described in *utmp*(4). The programs
     described in *acctcon*(1M) convert this file into session and charg-
     ing records, which are then summarized by *acctmerg*(1M).

     Process accounting is performed by the UNIX system kernel.
     Upon termination of a process, one record per process is written to
     a file (normally **/usr/adm/pacct**). The programs in *acctprc*(1M)
     summarize this data for charging purposes; *acctcms*(1M) is used
     to summarize command usage. Current process data may be
     examined using *acctcom*(1).

     Process accounting and connect time accounting (or any account-
     ing records in the format described in *acct*(4)) can be merged and
     summarized into total accounting records by *acctmerg* (see **tacct**
     format in *acct*(4)). *Prtacct* (see *acctsh*(1M)) is used to format
     any or all accounting records.

     Acctdisk reads lines that contain user ID, login name, and number
     of disk blocks and converts them to total accounting records that
     can be merged with other accounting records.

     Acctdusg reads its standard input (usually from **find / —print**)
     and computes disk resource consumption (including indirect
     blocks) by login. If **—u** is given, records consisting of those file
     names for which *acctdusg* charges no one are placed in *file* (a
     potential source for finding users trying to avoid disk charges). If
     —p is given, *file* is the name of the password file. This option is
     not needed if the password file is **/etc/passwd**.

Accton alone turns process accounting off. If *file* is given, it must be the name of an existing file, to which the kernel appends process accounting records (see *acct*(2) and *acct*(4)).

Acctwtmp writes a *utmp*(4) record to its standard output. The record contains the current time and a string of characters that describe the *reason*. A record type of ACCOUNTING is assigned (see *utmp*(4)). *Reason* must be a string of 11 or less characters, numbers, $, or spaces. For example, the following are suggestions for use in reboot and shutdown procedures, respectively:

          acctwtmp `uname` >> /etc/wtmp
          acctwtmp "file save" >> /etc/wtmp

FILES

/etc/passwd	used for login name to user ID conversions
/usr/lib/acct	holds all accounting commands listed in sub-class 1M of this manual
/usr/adm/pacct	current process accounting file
/etc/wtmp	login/logoff history file

SEE ALSO

acctcms(1M), acctcon(1M), acctmerg(1M), acctprc(1M), acctsh(1M), diskusg(1M), fwtmp(1M), runacct(1M).
acctcom(1) in the *UNIX Programmer's Manual—Volume 1: Commands and Utilities*.
acct(2), acct(4), utmp(4) in the *UNIX Programmer's Manual— Volume 2: System Calls and Library Routines*.

NAME

    acctcms – command summary from per-process accounting records

SYNOPSIS

    /usr/lib/acct/acctcms [options] files

DESCRIPTION

    Acctcms reads one or more *files*, normally in the form described in *acct*(4). It adds all records for processes that executed identically-named commands, sorts them, and writes them to the standard output, normally using an internal summary format. The *options* are:

    −a   Print output in ASCII rather than in the internal summary format. The output includes command name, number of times executed, total kcore-minutes, total CPU minutes, total real minutes, mean size (in K), mean CPU minutes per invocation, "hog factor", characters transferred, and blocks read and written, as in *acctcom*(1). Output is normally sorted by total kcore-minutes.

    −c   Sort by total CPU time, rather than total kcore-minutes.

    −j   Combine all commands invoked only once under "***other".

    −n   Sort by number of command invocations.

    −s   Any file names encountered hereafter are already in internal summary format.

    −t   Process all records as total accounting records. The default internal summary format splits each field into prime and non-prime time parts. This option combines the prime and non-prime time parts into a single field that is the total of both, and provides upward compatibility with old (i.e., UNIX System V) style **acctcms** internal summary format records.

    The following options may be used only with the -a option.

    −p   Output a prime-time-only command summary.

    −o   Output a non-prime (offshift) time only command summary.

    When −p and −o are used together, a combination prime and non-prime time report is produced. All the output summaries will be total usage except number of times executed, CPU minutes, and real minutes which will be split into prime and non-prime.

A typical sequence for performing daily command accounting and
for maintaining a running total is:

```
acctcms file ... >today
cp total previoustotal
acctcms −s today previoustotal >total
acctcms −a −s today
```

SEE ALSO

acct(1M),   acctcon(1M),   acctmerg(1M),   acctprc(1M),
acctsh(1M), fwtmp(1M), runacct(1M).
acctcom(1) in the *UNIX Programmer's Manual—Volume 1:
Commands and Utilities.*
acct(2), acct(4), utmp(4) in the *UNIX Programmer's Manual—
Volume 2: System Calls and Library Routines.*

BUGS

Unpredictable output results if −t is used on new style internal
summary format files, or if it is not used with old style internal
summary format files.

NAME
    acctcon1, acctcon2 — connect-time accounting

SYNOPSIS
    /usr/lib/acct/acctcon1 [options]

    /usr/lib/acct/acctcon2

DESCRIPTION
    Acctcon1 converts a sequence of login/logoff records read from its
    standard input to a sequence of records, one per login session. Its
    input should normally be redirected from **/etc/wtmp**. Its output is
    ASCII, giving device, user ID, login name, prime connect time
    (seconds), non-prime connect time (seconds), session starting time
    (numeric), and starting date and time. The *options* are:

    −p   Print input only, showing line name, login name, and time
             (in both numeric and date/time formats).

    −t   *Acctcon1* maintains a list of lines on which users are
             logged in. When it reaches the end of its input, it emits a
             session record for each line that still appears to be active.
             It normally assumes that its input is a current file, so that
             it uses the current time as the ending time for each ses-
             sion still in progress. The **−t** flag causes it to use,
             instead, the last time found in its input, thus assuring rea-
             sonable and repeatable numbers for non-current files.

    −l *file*   *File* is created to contain a summary of line usage show-
             ing line name, number of minutes used, percentage of
             total elapsed time used, number of sessions charged,
             number of logins, and number of logoffs. This file helps
             track line usage, identify bad lines, and find software and
             hardware oddities. Hang-up, termination of *login*(1) and
             termination of the login shell each generate logoff records,
             so that the number of logoffs is often three to four times
             the number of sessions. See *init*(1M) and *utmp*(4).

    −o *file*   *File* is filled with an overall record for the accounting
             period, giving starting time, ending time, number of
             reboots, and number of date changes.

    Acctcon2 expects as input a sequence of login session records and
    converts them into total accounting records (see **tacct** format in
    acct(4)).

EXAMPLES

These commands are typically used as shown below. The file **ctmp** is created only for the use of *acctprc* (1M) commands:

acctcon1 −t −l lineuse −o reboots <wtmp | sort +1n +2 >ctmp
acctcon2 <ctmp | acctmerg >ctacct

FILES

/etc/wtmp

SEE ALSO

acct(1M),   acctcms(1M),   acctmerg(1M),   acctprc(1M),
acctsh(1M), fwtmp(1M), init(1M), runacct(1M).
acctcom(1), login(1) in the *UNIX Programmer's Manual −
Volume 1: Commands and Utilities.*
acct(2), acct(4), utmp(4) in the *UNIX Programmer's Manual −
Volume 2: System Calls and Library Routines.*

BUGS

The line usage report is confused by date changes. Use *wtmpfix*
(see *fwtmp*(1M)) to correct this situation.

NAME

acctmerg — merge or add total accounting files

SYNOPSIS

/usr/lib/acct/acctmerg [options] [file] . . .

DESCRIPTION

Acctmerg reads its standard input and up to nine additional files, all in the **tacct** format (see *acct*(4)) or an ASCII version thereof. It merges these inputs by adding records whose keys (normally user ID and name) are identical, and expects the inputs to be sorted on those keys. *Options* are:

−**a**   Produce output in ASCII version of **tacct**.

−**i**   Input files are in ASCII version of **tacct**.

−**p**   Print input with no processing.

−**t**   Produce a single record that totals all input.

−**u**   Summarize by user ID, rather than user ID and name.

−**v**   Produce output in verbose ASCII format, with more precise notation for floating point numbers.

EXAMPLES

The following sequence is useful for making "repairs" to any file kept in this format:

        acctmerg −v <file1 >file2
                edit file2 as desired ...
        acctmerg −i <file2 >file1

SEE ALSO

acct(1M), acctcms(1M), acctcon(1M), acctprc(1M), acctsh(1M), fwtmp(1M), runacct(1M).

acctcom(1) in the *UNIX Programmer's Manual—Volume 1: Commands and Utilities.*

acct(2), acct(4), utmp(4) in the *UNIX Programmer's Manual— Volume 2: System Calls and Library Routines.*

NAME
  acctprc1, acctprc2 − process accounting

SYNOPSIS
  /usr/lib/acct/acctprc1 [ctmp]

  /usr/lib/acct/acctprc2

DESCRIPTION
  Acctprc1 reads input in the form described by *acct*(4), adds login names corresponding to user IDs, then writes for each process an ASCII line giving user ID, login name, prime CPU time (tics), non-prime CPU time (tics), and mean memory size (in memory segment units). If **ctmp** is given, it is expected to contain a list of login sessions, in the form described in *acctcon*(1M), sorted by user ID and login name. If this file is not supplied, it obtains login names from the password file. The information in **ctmp** helps it distinguish among different login names that share the same user ID.

  Acctprc2 reads records in the form written by *acctprc1*, summarizes them by user ID and name, then writes the sorted summaries to the standard output as total accounting records.

  These commands are typically used as shown below:

            acctprc1 ctmp </usr/adm/pacct | acctprc2 >ptacct

FILES
  /etc/passwd

SEE ALSO
  acct(1M),   acctcms(1M),   acctcon(1M),   acctmerg(1M),
  acctsh(1M), cron(1M), fwtmp(1M), runacct(1M).
  acctcom(1) in the *UNIX Programmer's Manual—Volume 1: Commands and Utilities*.
  acct(2), acct(4), utmp(4) in the *UNIX Programmer's Manual— Volume 2: System Calls and Library Routines*.

BUGS
  Although it is possible to distinguish among login names that share user IDs for commands run normally, it is difficult to do this for those commands run from *cron*(1M), for example. More precise conversion can be done by faking login sessions on the console via the *acctwtmp* program in *acct*(1M).

CAVEAT
A memory segment of the mean memory size is a unit of measure for the number of bytes in a logical memory segment on a particular processor.

NAME
>   chargefee, ckpacct, dodisk, lastlogin, monacct, nulladm, prctmp,
>   prdaily, prtacct, runacct, shutacct, startup, turnacct — shell pro-
>   cedures for accounting

SYNOPSIS
>   **/usr/lib/acct/chargefee** login-name number
>
>   **/usr/lib/acct/ckpacct** [blocks]
>
>   **/usr/lib/acct/dodisk** [-o] [files ...]
>
>   **/usr/lib/acct/lastlogin**
>
>   **/usr/lib/acct/monacct** number
>
>   **/usr/lib/acct/nulladm** file
>
>   **/usr/lib/acct/prctmp**
>
>   **/usr/lib/acct/prdaily** [-l] [-c] [mmdd]
>
>   **/usr/lib/acct/prtacct** file ["heading"]
>
>   **/usr/lib/acct/runacct** [mmdd] [mmdd state]
>
>   **/usr/lib/acct/shutacct** ["reason"]
>
>   **/usr/lib/acct/startup**
>
>   **/usr/lib/acct/turnacct on | off | switch**

DESCRIPTION
>   *Chargefee* can be invoked to charge a *number* of units to *login-
>   name*. A record is written to **/usr/adm/fee**, to be merged with
>   other accounting records during the night.
>
>   *Ckpacct* should be initiated via *cron*(1M). It periodically checks
>   the size of **/usr/adm/pacct**. If the size exceeds *blocks*, 1000 by
>   default, *turnacct* will be invoked with argument *switch*. If the
>   number of free disk blocks in the **/usr** file system falls below 500,
>   *ckpacct* will automatically turn off the collection of process
>   accounting records via the **off** argument to *turnacct*. When at
>   least this number of blocks is restored, the accounting will be
>   activated again. This feature is sensitive to the frequency at which
>   *ckpacct* is executed, usually by *cron*.
>
>   *Dodisk* should be invoked by *cron* to perform the disk accounting
>   functions. By default, it will do disk accounting on the special files
>   in **/etc/checklist**. If the **−o** flag is used, it will do a slower version
>   of disk accounting by login directory. *Files* specify the one or
>   more filesystem names where disk accounting will be done. If *files*

are used, disk accounting will be done on these filesystems only. If the −o flag is used, *files* should be mount points of mounted filesystem. If omitted, they should be the special file names of mountable filesystems.

Lastlogin is invoked by *runacct* to update **/usr/adm/acct/sum/loginlog**, which shows the last date on which each person logged in.

Monacct should be invoked once each month or each accounting period. *Number* indicates which month or period it is. If *number* is not given, it defaults to the current month (01−12). This default is useful if *monacct* is to executed via *cron*(1M) on the first day of each month. *Monacct* creates summary files in **/usr/adm/acct/fiscal** and restarts summary files in **/usr/adm/acct/sum**.

Nulladm creates *file* with mode 664 and insures that owner and group are **adm**. It is called by various accounting shell procedures.

Prctmp can be used to print the session record file (normally **/usr/adm/acct/nite/ctmp** created by *acctcon1* (see *acctcon*(1M)).

Prdaily is invoked by *runacct* to format a report of the previous day's accounting data. The report resides in **/usr/adm/acct/sum/rprt***mmdd* where *mmdd* is the month and day of the report. The current daily accounting reports may be printed by typing *prdaily*. Previous days' accounting reports can be printed by using the *mmdd* option and specifying the exact report date desired. The −l flag prints a report of exceptional usage by login id for the specifed date. Previous daily reports are cleaned up and therefore inaccessible after each invocation of *monacct*. The −c flag prints a report of exceptional resource usage by command, and may be used on current day's accounting data only.

Prtacct can be used to format and print any total accounting (**tacct**) file.

Runacct performs the accumulation of connect, process, fee, and disk accounting on a daily basis. It also creates summaries of command usage. For more information, see *runacct*(1M).

Shutacct should be invoked during a system shutdown (usually in **/etc/shutdown**) to turn process accounting off and append a "reason" record to **/etc/wtmp**.

Startup should be called by **/etc/rc** to turn the accounting on whenever the system is brought up.

Turnacct is an interface to *accton* (see *acct*(1M)) to turn process accounting **on** or **off**. The **switch** argument turns accounting off, moves the current **/usr/adm/pacct** to the next free name in **/usr/adm/pacct***incr* (where *incr* is a number starting with **1** and incrementing by one for each additional **pacct** file), then turns accounting back on again. This procedure is called by *ckpacct* and thus can be taken care of by the *cron* and used to keep **pacct** to a reasonable size.

FILES

/usr/adm/fee	accumulator for fees
/usr/adm/pacct	current file for per-process accounting
/usr/adm/pacct*	used if pacct gets large and during execution of daily accounting procedure
/etc/wtmp	login/logoff summary
/usr/lib/acct/ptelus.awk	contains the limits for exceptional usage by login id
/usr/lib/acct/ptecms.awk	contains the limits for exceptional usage by command name
/usr/adm/acct/nite	working directory
/usr/lib/acct	holds all accounting commands listed in sub-class 1M of this manual
/usr/adm/acct/sum	summary directory, should be saved

SEE ALSO

acct(1M),   acctcms(1M),   acctcon(1M),   acctmerg(1M), acctprc(1M), cron(1M), diskusg(1M), fwtmp(1M), runacct(1M). acctcom(1) in the *UNIX Programmer's Manual—Volume 1: Commands and Utilities.* acct(2), acct(4), utmp(4) in the *UNIX Programmer's Manual— Volume 2: System Calls and Library Routines.*

NAME
　　bcopy − interactive block copy

SYNOPSIS
　　/etc/bcopy

DESCRIPTION
　　Bcopy dates from a time when neither the UNIX system file nor the disk drives were as reliable as they are now. *Bcopy* copies from and to files starting at arbitrary block (512-byte) boundaries.

　　The following questions are asked:

> **to:** (you name the file or device to be copied to).
> **offset:** (you provide the starting "to" block number).
> **from:** (you name the file or device to be copied from).
> **offset:** (you provide the starting "from" block number).
> **count:** (you reply with the number of blocks to be copied).

　　After **count** is exhausted, the **from** question is repeated (giving you a chance to concatenate blocks at the **to+offset+count** location). If you answer **from** with a carriage return, everything starts over.

　　Two consecutive carriage returns terminate *bcopy*.

SEE ALSO
　　cpio(1), dd(1) in the *UNIX Programmer's Manual−Volume 1: Commands and Utilities*.

NAME
    bdblk - print, initialize, update or recover bad sector information
    on disk packs

SYNOPSIS
    /etc/bdblk option unit [sector ...]

DESCRIPTION
    Bdblk can be used to print, initialize, update or recover the bad
    block information stored on disk that is used by the disk drivers to
    implement bad sector replacement.

    The bad sector information on 3B20 computer is located in the last
    sector of the first cylinder of the disk pack.

    Replacement sectors are allocated starting with the first sector
    before the bad sector information and working backwards toward
    the beginning of the disk. A maximum of 126 bad sectors are sup-
    ported. The position of the bad sector in the bad sector table
    determines which replacement sector it corresponds to.

    The bad sector information structure is as follows:

    struct badblk {
            int bb_magic;   /* bad block information magic # */
            int bb_count;   /* number of bad sectors in table */
            daddr bb_blkno[126]; /* sector number of bad sector */
    };

    Bdblk is invoked by giving an *option* and the *unit* number of the
    disk drive number. The *option* is specified by one of the following
    letters:

    p   It reads the bad sector information from the specified
            unit and prints out the bad sector information.

    i   It verifies the format of the specified unit and initial-
            izes the bad sector information on disk.

    u   It verifies the format of the specified unit and updates
            the bad sector information on disk.

    r   It may be invoked by giving a list of bad sectors. It
            will then write the supplied information onto the disk.
            This option should only be used to restore known bad
            sector information which was destroyed.

WARNINGS
>   After having changed the bad sector information on disk, the disk
>   should be put out of service to insure the system bad block infor-
>   mation table for that unit is current.

NAME
     brc, bcheckrc, rc, powerfail — system initialization shell scripts

SYNOPSIS
     /etc/brc

     /etc/bcheckrc

     /etc/rc

     /etc/powerfail

DESCRIPTION
     Except for *powerfail*, these shell procedures are executed via
     entries in **/etc/inittab** by *init*(1M) when the system is changed out
     of *SINGLE USER* mode. *Powerfail* is executed whenever a system
     power failure is detected.

     The *brc* procedure clears the mounted file system table,
     /etc/mnttab (see *mnttab*(4)), and loads any programmable micro-
     processors with their appropriate scripts.

     The *bcheckrc* procedure performs all the necessary consistency
     checks to prepare the system to change into multi-user mode. It
     will prompt to set the system date and to check the file systems
     with *fsck*(1M).

     The *rc* procedure starts all system daemons before the terminal
     lines are enabled for multi-user mode. In addition, file systems are
     mounted and accounting, error logging, system activity logging and
     the Remote Job Entry (RJE) system are activated in this pro-
     cedure.

     The *powerfail* procedure is invoked when the system detects a
     power failure condition. Its chief duty is to reload any programm-
     able micro-processors with their appropriate scripts, if suitable. It
     also logs the fact that a power failure occurred.

     These shell procedures, in particular *rc* may be used for several
     run-level states. The *who*(1) command may be used to get the
     run-level information.

SEE ALSO
     fsck(1M), init(1M), shutdown(1M).
     who(1) in the *UNIX Programmer's Manual—Volume 1: Com-
     mands and Utilities*.
     inittab(4), mnttab(4) in the *UNIX Programmer's Manual—
     Volume 2: System Calls and Library Routines*.

NAME
> checkall — faster file system checking procedure

SYNOPSIS
> **/etc/checkall**

DESCRIPTION
> The *checkall* procedure is a prototype and must be modified to suit local conditions. The following will serve as an example:

>> # check the root file system by itself
>> fsck /dev/dsk/0s0

>> # dual fsck of drives 0 and 1
>> dfsck /dev/rdsk/0s[12345] — /dev/rdsk/1s1

> In the above example (where **/dev/rdsk/1s1** is 320K blocks and **/dev/rdsk/0s[12345]** are each 65K or less), a previous sequential *fsck* took 19 minutes. The *checkall* procedure takes 11 minutes.

> *Dfsck* is a program that permits an operator to interact with two *fsck*(1M) programs at once. To aid in this, *dfsck* will print the file system name for each message to the operator. When answering a question from *dfsck*, the operator must prefix the response with a **1** or a **2** (indicating that the answer refers to the first or second file system group).

> Due to the file system load balancing required for dual checking, the *dfsck* command should always be executed through the *checkall* shell procedure.

> In a practical sense, the file systems are divided as follows:

>> dfsck file_systems_on_drive_0 — file_systems_on_drive_1
>> dfsck file_systems_on_drive_2 — file_systems_on_drive_3
>> . . .

> A three-drive system can be handled by this more concrete example (assumes two large file systems per drive):

>> dfsck /dev/dsk/3s1 /dev/dsk/0s[14] — /dev/dsk/1s[14] /dev/dsk/3s4

> Note that the first file system on drive 3 is first in the *filesystems1* list and is last in the *filesystems2* list assuring that references to that drive will not overlap at execution time.

WARNINGS

1. Do not use *dfsck* to check the *root* file system.

2. On a check that requires a scratch file (see −t above), be careful not to use the same temporary file for the two groups (this is sure to scramble the file systems).

3. The *dfsck* procedure is useful only if the system is set up for multiple physical I/O buffers.

SEE ALSO

fsck(1M).

NAME
     chroot — change root directory for a command

SYNOPSIS
     /etc/chroot newroot command

DESCRIPTION
     The given command is executed *relative to the new root*. The
     meaning of any initial slashes (/) in path names is changed for a
     command and any of its children to *newroot*. Furthermore, the
     initial working directory is *newroot*.

     Notice that:

               chroot newroot command >x

     will create the file **x** relative to the original root, not the new one.

     This command is restricted to the super-user.

     The new root path name is always relative to the current root:
     even if a *chroot* is currently in effect, the *newroot* argument is
     relative to the current root of the running process.

SEE ALSO
     chdir(2) in the *UNIX Programmer's Manual—Volume 2: System
     Calls and Library Routines*.

BUGS
     One should exercise extreme caution when referencing special files
     in the new root file system.

NAME
     clri — clear i-node

SYNOPSIS
     /etc/clri file-system i-number ...

DESCRIPTION
     Clri writes zeros on the 64 bytes occupied by the i-node numbered
     i-number. *File-system* must be a special file name referring to a
     device containing a file system. After *clri* is executed, any blocks
     in the affected file will show up as "missing" in an *fsck*(1M) of
     the *file-system*. This command should only be used in emergen-
     cies and extreme care should be exercised.

     Read and write permission is required on the specified *file-system*
     device. The i-node becomes allocatable.

     The primary purpose of this routine is to remove a file which for
     some reason appears in no directory. If it is used to *zap* an i-node
     which does appear in a directory, care should be taken to track
     down the entry and remove it. Otherwise, when the i-node is real-
     located to some new file, the old entry will still point to that file.
     At that point removing the old entry will destroy the new file. The
     new entry will again point to an unallocated i-node, so the whole
     cycle is likely to be repeated again and again.

SEE ALSO
     fsck(1M), fsdb(1M), ncheck(1M).
     fs(4) in the *UNIX Programmer's Manual —Volume 2: System
     Calls and Library Routines*.

BUGS
     If the file is open, *clri* is likely to be ineffective.

NAME

    config — configure a UNIX system

SYNOPSIS

    /etc/config [−n] [−t] [−l file] [−c file] [−m file]
    dfile

DESCRIPTION

    Config is a program that takes a description of a UNIX system and generates two files. One file provides information regarding the interface between the hardware and device handlers. The other file is a C program defining the configuration tables for the various devices on the system.

    The **−n** option produces a non-separated **I** and **low.s** core image for some computers (this is for small systems, i.e., PDP11/23 and 11/34).

    The **−l** option specifies the name of the hardware interface file; **low.s** is the default name on some small computers; **univec.c** is the default name on most larger computers.

    The **−c** option specifies the name of the configuration table file; **conf.c** is the default name.

    The **−m** option specifies the name of the file that contains all the information regarding supported devices; **/etc/master** is the default name. This file is supplied with the UNIX system and should *not* be modified unless the user *fully* understands its construction.

    The **−t** option requests a short table of major device numbers for character and block type devices. This can facilitate the creation of special files.

    The user must supply *dfile*; it must contain device information for the user's system. This file is divided into two parts. The first part contains physical device specifications. The second part contains system-dependent information. Any line with an asterisk (•) in column 1 is a comment.

    In the following, all configurations are assumed to have the following devices:

        one DL11 (for the system console)
        one KW11-L line clock or KW11-P programmable clock

    with standard interrupt vectors and addresses. These two devices *must not* be specified in *dfile*. Note that the UNIX operating system needs only one clock, but can handle both types.

First Part of *dfile*

Each line contains up to six fields, delimited by blanks and/or tabs in the following format:

devname   vector   address   bus   number   nexus

where *devname* is the name of the device (as it appears in the **/etc/master** device table), *vector* is the interrupt vector location (octal), *address* is the device address (octal), *bus* is the bus request level (4 through 7), *number* is the number (decimal) of devices associated with the corresponding controller, and *nexus* is the nexus number of the UNIBUS adapter (VAX-11/780 only) associated with this device. *Number* is optional, and if omitted, a default value which is the maximum value for that controller is used. *Nexus* is optional, and if omitted, a default value appropriate for each machine type will be used. If *nexus* is specified, then *number* must be specified as well.

There are certain drivers that may be provided with the system, that are actually *pseudo-device* drivers; that is, there is no real hardware associated with the driver. Drivers of this type are identified on their respective manual entries. When these devices are specified in the description file, the interrupt *vector*, device *address*, and *bus* request level must all be zero.

If the device is a VAX-11 massbus adapter, then *vector* is the adapter nexus number, and *address* must be zero.

Second Part of *dfile*

The second part contains three different types of lines. Note that *all* specifications of this part *are required*, although their order is arbitrary.

1. *Root/pipe/dump device specification*

   Three lines of three fields each:

root	devname	minor
pipe	devname	minor
dump	devname	minor

   where *minor* is the minor device number (in octal).

2. *Swap device specification*

One line that contains five fields as follows:

      swap   devname   minor swplo nswap

where *swplo* is the lowest disk block (decimal) in the swap area and *nswap* is the number of disk blocks (decimal) in the swap area.

3. *Parameter specification*

Several lines of two fields each as follows (*number* is decimal):

buffers	number	
sabufs	number	(zero on the VAX-11)
i-nodes	number	
files	number	
mounts	number	
coremap	number	(PDP-11 only)
swapmap	number	
calls	number	
procs	number	
maxproc	number	
texts	number	
clists	number	
hashbuf	number	
physbuf	number	
x25links	number	
x25bufs	number	
x25map	number	
x25bytes	number	
iblocks	number	(PDP-11 only)
power	0 or 1	
mesg	0 or 1	
sema	0 or 1	
shmem	0 or 1	(VAX-11 only)
maus	0 or 1	(PDP-11 only)

EXAMPLE

To configure a PDP-11/70 system with the following devices:
one RP06 disk drive controller with 6 drives
one DH11 asynchronous multiplexer with 16 lines (default number)
one DM11 modem control with 16 lines (for the DH11)
one DH11 asynchronous multiplexer with 8 lines
one DM11 modem control with 8 lines (for the DH11)

one LP11 line printer
one TU16 tape drive controller with 2 drives
one DL11 asynchronous interface

Note that the UNIX system only supports DH11 units that require corresponding DM11 units. It is wise to specify them in DH-DM pairs to facilitate understanding the configuration. Note also that, in the preceding case, the DL11 that is specified is *in addition* to the DL11 that was part of the initial system. We must also specify the following parameter information:

root device is an RP06 (drive 0, section 0)
pipe device is an RP06 (drive 0, section 0)
swap device is an RP06 (drive 1, section 4),
        with a swplo of 6000 and an nswap of 2000
dump device is a TU16 (drive 0)
number of buffers is 35
number of *system addressable* buffers is 12
number of processes is 150
maximum number of processes per user ID is 25
number of mounts is 8
number of i-nodes is 120
number of files is 120
number of calls is 30
number of texts is 35
number of character buffers is 150
number of coremap entries is 50
number of swapmap entries is 50
power fail recovery is to be included
messages are to be included
semaphores are to be included
one pseudo device driver for the Operating System Profiler

The actual system configuration would be specified as follows:

rp06	254	776700	5	6
dh11	320	760020	5	
dm11	300	770500	4	
dh11	330	760060	5	8
dm11	304	770510	4	8
lp11	200	775514	5	
tu16	224	772440	5	2
dl11	350	775610	5	
prf	0	0	0	
root	rp06	0		

pipe	rp06	0		
swap	rp06	14	6000	2000
dump	tu16	0		

* Comments may be inserted in this manner

buffers	35
sabufs	12
procs	150
maxproc	25
mounts	8
i-nodes	120
files	120
calls	30
texts	35
clists	150
coremap	50
swapmap	50
power	1
msg	1
sema	1

FILES

/etc/master	default input master device table
low.s	default output hardware interface file for PDP-11
univec.c	default output hardware interface file for the VAX-11
conf.c	default output configuration table file

SEE ALSO

sysdef(1M).

master(4) in the *UNIX Programmer's Manual—Volume 2: System Calls and Library Routines.*

DIAGNOSTICS

Diagnostics are routed to the standard output and are self-explanatory.

BUGS

The −t option does not know about devices that have aliases. For example, a TE16 (an alias for a TU16) will show up as a TU16; however, the major device numbers are always correct.

NAME
>   cpset — install object files in binary directories

SYNOPSIS
>   **cpset [-o]** object directory [mode owner group]

DESCRIPTION
>   *Cpset* is used to install the specified *object* file in the given *directory*. The *mode*, *owner*, and *group*, of the destination file may be specified on the command line. If this data is omitted, two results are possible:
>
>> If the user of *cpset* has administrative permissions (that is, the user's numerical ID is less than 100), the following defaults are provided:
>>
>>> mode — 0755
>>>
>>> owner — bin
>>>
>>> group — bin
>>
>> If the user is not an administrator, the default, owner, and group of the destination file will be that of the invoker.
>
>   An optional argument of −**o** will force *cpset* to move *object* to **OLD***object* in the destination directory before installing the new object.
>
>   For example:
>
>> cpset echo /bin 0755 bin bin
>>
>> cpset echo /bin
>>
>> cpset echo /bin/echo
>
>   All the examples above have the same effect (assuming the user is an administrator). The file **echo** will be copied into **/bin** and will be given **0755, bin, bin** as the mode, owner, and group, respectively.
>
>   *Cpset* utilizes the file **/usr/src/destinations** to determine the final destination of a file. The locations file contains pairs of path names separated by spaces or tabs. The first name is the "official" destination (for example: **/bin/echo**). The second name is the new destination. For example, if *echo* is moved from **/bin** to **/usr/bin**, the entry in **/usr/src/destinations** would be:
>
>> /bin/echo   /usr/bin/echo

When the actual installation happens, *cpset* verifies that the "old" path name does not exist. If a file exists at that location, *cpset* issues a warning and continues. This file does not exist on a distribution tape; it is used by sites to track local command movement. The procedures used to build the source will be responsible for defining the "official" locations of the source.

Cross Generation

The environment variable **ROOT** will be used to locate the destination file (in the form **$ROOT/usr/src/destinations**). This is necessary in the cases where cross generation is being done on a production system.

SEE ALSO

install(1M), mk(8).

make(1) in the *UNIX Programmer's Manual—Volume 1: Commands and Utilities*.

NAME
    crash — examine system images
SYNOPSIS
    /etc/crash [system] [namelist]
DESCRIPTION
    Crash is an interactive utility for examining an operating system
    core image. It has facilities for interpreting and formatting the
    various control structures in the system and certain miscellaneous
    functions that are useful when perusing a dump.

    The arguments to *crash* are the file name where the *system* image
    can be found and a *namelist* file to be used for symbol values.

    The default values are **/dev/mem** and **/unix**; hence, *crash* with no
    arguments can be used to examine an active system. If a *system*
    image file is given, it is assumed to be a system core dump and the
    default process is set to be that of the process running at the time
    of the crash. This is determined by a value stored in a fixed loca-
    tion by the dump mechanism.

COMMANDS
    Input to *crash* is typically of the form:
                command [*options*] [structures to be printed].
    When allowed, *options* will modify the format of the printout. If
    no specific structure elements are specified, all valid entries will be
    used. As an example, **proc** — **12 15 3** would print process table
    slots 12, 15, and 3 in a long format, while **proc** would print the
    entire process table in standard format.

    In general, those commands that perform I/O with addresses
    assume hexadecimal on 32-bit machines and octal on 16-bit
    machines.

    The current repertory consists of:

    user [list of process table entries]
            Aliases: **uarea, u_area, u**.
            Print the user structure of the named process as deter-
            mined by the information contained in the process table
            entry. If no entry number is given, the information from
            the last executing process will be printed. Swapped
            processes produce an error message.

    trace —r [list of process table entries]
            Aliases: **t —r**.
            Generate a kernel stack trace of the current process. The
UNIX Programmer's Manual   System Administration Facilities—31

trace begins at the saved stack frame pointer in **kfp**. If no
entry number is given, the information from the last executing process will be printed.

kfp [stack frame pointer]
    Aliases: **r5, fp**.
    Print the program's idea of the start of the current stack
    frame (set initially from a fixed location in the dump) if
    no argument is given, or set the frame pointer to the sup-
    plied value.

stack [list of process table entries]
    Aliases: **stk, s, kernel, k**.
    Format a dump of the kernel stack of a process. The
    addresses shown are virtual system data addresses rather
    than true physical locations. If no entry number is given,
    the information from the last executing process will be
    printed.

proc [−[r]] [list of process table entries]
    Aliases: **ps, p**.
    Format the process table. The −r option causes only
    runnable processes to be printed. The − alone generates
    a longer listing.

pcb [list of process table entries]
    Print the process control block of the current process. If
    no entry number is given, the information from the last
    executing process will be printed.

inode [−] [list of i-node table entries]
    Aliases: **ino, i**.
    Format the i-node table. The − option will also print the
    i-node data block addresses.

file [list of file table entries]
    Aliases: **files, f**.
    Format the file table.

lck
    Aliases: **l**
    Print the active and sleep record lock tables; also verify
    the correctness of the record locking linked lists.

mount [list of mount table entries]
> Aliases: **mnt, m.**
> Format the mount table.

text [list of text table entries]
> Aliases: **txt, x.**
> Format the text table.

tty [type] [−] [list of tty entries]
> Aliases: **term**
> Print the tty structures. The *type* argument determines
> which structure will be used (such as **tn83, tn74,** or **tn4** on
> the 3B20 computers). No default *type* is provided. How-
> ever, once specified, the last *type* is remembered. The −
> option prints the *stty*(1) parameters for the given line.

stat
> Print certain statistics found in the dump. These include
> the panic string (if a panic occurred), time of crash, sys-
> tem name, and the registers saved in low memory by the
> dump mechanism.

var
> Aliases: **tunables, tunable, tune, v.**
> Print the tunable system parameters.

buf [list of buffer headers]
> Aliases: **hdr, bufhdr.**
> Format the system buffer headers.

buffer [format] [list of buffers]
> Alias: **b.**
> Print the data in a system buffer according to *format*. If
> *format* is omitted, the previous *format* is used. Valid for-
> mats include **decimal, octal, hex, character, byte, directory,
> i-node,** and **write.** The last creates a file in the current
> directory (see *FILES*) containing the buffer data.

callout Aliases: **calls, call, c, timeout, time, tout.**
> Print all entries in the callout table.

region [region table number | region table address]
> Prints region table. Region table address must be of the
> form 0x ... .

preg [proc slot number]
> Prints data about a process's pregions.

map [list of map names]
> Format the named system map structures.

nm [list of symbols]
> Print symbol value and type as found in the *namelist* file.

ts [list of text addresses]
> Find the closest text symbols to the given addresses.

ds [list of data addresses]
> Find the closest data symbols to the given addresses.

od [symbol name or address] [count] [format]
> Aliases: **dump, rd**.
> Dump *count* data values starting at the symbol value or
> address given according to *format*. Allowable formats are
> **octal, longoct, decimal, longdec, character, hex,** or **byte**.

semalog [n]
> Alias: **slog**.
> Print the log of semaphore activity. It is printed in chrono-
> logical order. The optional numeric argument is used to
> request the n most recent entries. If the argument is
> omitted, the entire log is printed.

!   Escape to shell.

q   Exit from *crash*.

?   Print synopsis of commands.

ALIASES
> There are built-in aliases for many of the *formats* as well as those
> listed for the commands. Some of them are:

byte	b.
character	char, c.
decimal	dec, e.
directory	direct, dir, d.
hexadecimal	hexadec, hex, h, x.
i-node	ino , i.
longdec	ld, D.
longoct	lo, O.
octal	oct, o.
write	w.

FILES

/usr/include/sys/*.h header files for table and structure info
/dev/mem   default system image file
/unix   default namelist file
buf.#   files created containing buffer data

SEE ALSO

mount(1M).

nm(1), ps(1), sh(1), stty(1) in the *UNIX Programmer's Manual—Volume 1: Commands and Utilities.*

BUGS

Most flags are abbreviated and will have little meaning to the uninitiated user. A source listing of the system header files at hand would be most useful while using *crash.*

Stack tracing of the current process on a running system and procs running at the time of a crash do not work.

NAME
cron - clock daemon

SYNOPSIS
/etc/cron

DESCRIPTION
Cron executes commands at specified dates and times. Regularly scheduled commands can be specified according to instructions found in crontab files; users can submit their own crontab file via the *crontab* command. Commands which are to be executed only once may be submitted via the *at* command. Since *cron* never exits, it should only be executed once. This is best done by running *cron* from the initialization process through the file **/etc/rc**.

Cron only examines crontab files and at command files during process initialization and when a file changes. This reduces the overhead of checking for new or changed files at regularly scheduled intervals.

FILES
/usr/lib/cron	main cron directory
/usr/lib/cron/log	accounting information
/usr/spool/cron	spool area

SEE ALSO
at(1), crontab(1), sh(1) in the *UNIX Programmer's Manual — Volume 1: Commands and Utilities.*

DIAGNOSTICS
A history of all actions taken by cron are recorded in **/usr/lib/cron/log**.

NAME
    dcopy — copy file systems for optimal access time

SYNOPSIS
    /etc/dcopy [−s*X*] [−a*n*] [−d] [−v] [−f*fsize*[:*isize*]] inputfs
    outputfs

DESCRIPTION
    Dcopy copies file system *inputfs* to *outputfs*. *Inputfs* is the exist-
    ing file system; *outputfs* is an appropriately sized file system, to
    hold the reorganized result. For best results *inputfs* should be the
    raw device and *outputfs* should be the block device. *Dcopy* should
    be run on unmounted file systems (in the case of the root file sys-
    tem, copy to a new pack). With no arguments, *dcopy* copies files
    from *inputfs* compressing directories by removing vacant entries,
    and spacing consecutive blocks in a file by the optimal rotational
    gap. The possible options are

    −s*X*   supply device information for creating an optimal
               organization of blocks in a file. The forms of *X* are the
               same as the −s option of *fsck* (1M).

    −a*n*   place the files not accessed in *n* days after the free
               blocks of the destination file system (default for *n* is 7).
               If no *n* is specified then no movement occurs.

    −d   leave order of directory entries as is (default is to move
               sub-directories to the beginning of directories).

    −v   currently reports how many files were processed, and
               how big the source and destination freelists are.

    −f*fsize*[:*isize*]
               specify the *outputfs* file system and inode list sizes (in
               blocks). If the option (or :*isize*) is not given, the
               values from the *inputfs* are used.

    Dcopy catches interrupts and quits and reports on its progress. To
    terminate *dcopy* send a quit signal, and *dcopy* will no longer catch
    interrupts or quits.

SEE ALSO
    fsck(1M), mkfs(1M).
    ps(1) in the *UNIX Programmer's Manual —Volume 1: Commands
    and Utilities.*

NAME
     devnm — device name

SYNOPSIS
     /etc/devnm [names]

DESCRIPTION
     Devnm identifies the special file associated with the mounted file
     system where the argument *name* resides. (As a special case, both
     the block device name and the swap device name are printed for
     the argument name **/** if swapping is done on the same disk section
     as the **root** file system.) Argument names must be full path
     names.

     This command is most commonly used by **/etc/rc** (see *brc* (1M))
     to construct a mount table entry for the **root** device.

EXAMPLE
     The command:
             /etc/devnm /usr
     produces
             dsk/0s1 /usr
     if **/usr** is mounted on **/dev/dsk/0s1**.

FILES
     /dev/dsk/*
     /etc/mnttab

SEE ALSO
     brc(1M), setmnt(1M).

NAME
  df — report number of free disk blocks

SYNOPSIS
  df [−t] [−f] [file-systems]

DESCRIPTION
  Df prints out the number of free blocks and free i-nodes available
  for on-line file systems by examining the counts kept in the super-
  blocks; *file-systems* may be specified either by device name (e.g.,
  /dev/dsk/0s1) or by mounted directory name (e.g., **/usr**). If the
  file-systems argument is unspecified, the free space on all of the
  mounted file systems is printed.

  The −t flag causes the total allocated block figures to be reported
  as well.

  If the −f flag is given, only an actual count of the blocks in the
  free list is made (free i-nodes are not reported). With this option,
  df will report on raw devices.

FILES
  /dev/dsk/*
  /etc/mnttab

SEE ALSO
  fs(4), mnttab(4) in the *UNIX Programmer's Manual—Volume 2:
  System Calls and Library Routines.*

NAME

   diskusg - generate disk accounting data by user ID

SYNOPSIS

   diskusg [options] [files]

DESCRIPTION

   Diskusg generates intermediate disk accounting information from
   data in *files,* or the standard input if omitted. *Diskusg* output
   lines on the standard output, one per user, in the following format:

   > *uid login #blocks*

   where

   uid -   the numerical user ID of the user.

   login -   the login name of the user; and

   #blocks -   the total number of disk blocks allocated to this user.

   Diskusg normally reads only the i-nodes of file systems for disk
   accounting. In this case, *files* are the special filenames of these
   devices.

   Diskusg recognizes the following options:

   -s   the input data is already in *diskusg* output format.
                  Diskusg combines all lines for a single user into a
                  single line.

   -v   verbose. Print a list on standard error of all files
                  that are charged to no one.

   -i *fnmlist*   ignore the data on those file systems whose file sys-
                  tem name is in *fnmlist. Fnmlist* is a list of file sys-
                  tem names separated by commas or enclose within
                  quotes. *Diskusg* compares each name in this list
                  with the file system name stored in the volume ID.

   -p *file*   use *file* as the name of the password file to generate
                  login names. **/etc/passwd** is used by default.

   -u *file*   write records to *file* of files that are charged to no
                  one. Records consist of the special file name, the i-
                  node number, and the user ID.

The output of *diskusg* is normally the input to *acctdisk* (see *acct*(1M)) which generates total accounting records that can be merged with other accounting records. *Diskusg* is normally run in *dodisk* (see *acctsh*(1M)).

EXAMPLES

The following will generate daily disk accounting information:

```
for i in /dev/rp00 /dev/rp01 /dev/rp10 /dev/rp11; do
        diskusg $i > dtmp.'basename $i' &
done
wait
diskusg -s dtmp.* | sort +0n +1 | acctdisk > disktacct
```

FILES

/etc/passwd   used for user ID to login name conversions

SEE ALSO

acct(1M), acctsh(1M).
acct(4) in the *UNIX Programmer's Manual—Volume 2: System Calls and Library Routines.*

NAME
    errdead — extract error records from dump

SYNOPSIS
    /etc/errdead dumpfile [namelist]

DESCRIPTION
    When hardware errors are detected by the system, an error record
    that contains information pertinent to the error is generated. If
    the error-logging daemon *errdemon*(1M) is not active or if the
    system crashes before the record can be placed in the error file, the
    error information is held by the system in a local buffer. *Errdead*
    examines a system dump (or memory), extracts such error records,
    and passes them to *errpt*(1M) for analysis.

    The *dumpfile* specifies the file (or memory) that is to be examined.
    The system namelist is specified by *namelist*; if not given, **/unix** is
    used.

FILES
    /unix   system namelist
    /usr/bin/errpt   analysis program
    /usr/tmp/errXXXXXX temporary file

DIAGNOSTICS
    Diagnostics may come from either *errdead* or *errpt*. In either
    case, they are intended to be self-explanatory.

SEE ALSO
    errdemon(1M), errpt(1M).

NAME
errdemon — error-logging daemon

SYNOPSIS
/usr/lib/errdemon [file]

DESCRIPTION
The error logging daemon *errdemon* collects error records from
the operating system by reading the special file **/dev/error** and
places them in *file*. If *file* is not specified when the daemon is
activated, **/usr/adm/errfile** is used. Note that *file* is created if it
does not exist; otherwise, error records are appended to it, so that
no previous error data is lost. No analysis of the error records is
done by *errdemon*; that responsibility is left to *errpt*(1M). The
error-logging daemon is terminated by sending it a software kill
signal (see *kill*(1)). Only the super-user may start the daemon,
and only one daemon may be active at any time.

FILES
/dev/error   source of error records
/usr/adm/errfile   repository for error records

DIAGNOSTICS
The diagnostics produced by *errdemon* are intended to be self-
explanatory.

SEE ALSO
errpt(1M), errstop(1M), err(7).
kill(1) in the *UNIX Programmer's Manual—Volume 1: Commands and Utilities*.

NAME

errpt — process a report of logged errors

SYNOPSIS

errpt [options] [files]

DESCRIPTION

Errpt processes data collected by the error logging mechanism (*errdemon*(1M)) and generates a report of that data. The default report is a summary of all errors posted in the files named. Options apply to all files and are described below. If no files are specified, *errpt* attempts to use **/usr/adm/errfile** as *file*.

A summary report notes the options that may limit its completeness, records the time stamped on the earliest and latest errors encountered, and gives the total number of errors of one or more types. Each device summary contains the total number of unrecovered errors, recovered errors, errors unable to be logged, I/O operations on the device, and miscellaneous activities that occurred on the device. The number of times that *errpt* has difficulty reading input data is included as read errors.

Any detailed report contains, in addition to specific error information, all instances of the error logging process being started and stopped, and any time changes (via *date*(1)) that took place during the interval being processed. A summary of each error type included in the report is appended to a detailed report.

A report may be limited to certain records in the following ways:

−s *date* Ignore all records posted earlier than *date*, where *date* has the form *mmddhhmmyy*, consistent in meaning with the *date*(1) command.

−e *date* Ignore all records posted later than *date*, whose form is as described above.

−a Produce a detailed report that includes all error types.

−d *devlist* A detailed report is limited to data about devices given in *devlist*, where *devlist* can be one of two forms: a list of device identifiers separated from one another by a comma, or a list of device identifiers enclosed in double quotes and separated from one another by a comma and/or more spaces. *Errpt* is familiar with the common form of identifiers. For the 3B20 computer the devices for which errors are logged are DFC, IOP, and MT. For Digital Equipment Corporation machines, the (block) devices for which errors are logged are RP03, RP04, RP05, RP06, RP07, RS03, RS04, TS11, TU10, TU16, TU78, RK05, RK06, RK07, RM05, RM80, and RF11. Additional identifiers are **int** and **mem** which include detailed reports of stray-interrupt and memory-parity type errors, respectively.

−**p** *n*   Limit the size of a detailed report to *n* pages.

−**f**   In a detailed report, limit the reporting of block device errors to unrecovered errors.

FILES

/usr/adm/errfile   default error file

SEE ALSO

errdead(1M), errdemon(1M).

date(1) in the *UNIX Programmer's Manual—Volume 1: Commands and Utilities.*

errfile(4) in the *UNIX Programmer's Manual—Volume 2: System Calls and Library Routines.*

NAME
errstop − terminate the error-logging daemon

SYNOPSIS
/etc/errstop [namelist]

DESCRIPTION
The error-logging daemon *errdemon*(1M) is terminated by using *errstop*. This is accomplished by executing *ps*(1) to determine the daemon's identity and then sending it a software kill signal (see *signal*(2)); **/unix** is used as the system namelist if none is specified. Only the super-user may use *errstop*.

FILES
/unix   default system namelist

DIAGNOSTICS
The diagnostics produced by *errstop* are intended to be self-explanatory.

SEE ALSO
errdemon(1M).

ps(1) in the *UNIX Programmer's Manual−Volume 1: Commands and Utilities*.

kill(2), signal(2) in the *UNIX Programmer's Manual−Volume 2: System Calls and Library Routines*.

NAME
     ff − list file names and statistics for a file system

SYNOPSIS
     /etc/ff [options] special

DESCRIPTION
     Ff reads the i-list and directories of the *special* file, assuming it to
     be a file system, saving i-node data for files which match the selec-
     tion criteria. Output consists of the path name for each saved i-
     node, plus any other file information requested using the print
     options below. Output fields are positional. The output is pro-
     duced in i-node order; fields are separated by tabs. The default
     line produced by *ff* is:

              path-name i-number

     With all *options* enabled, output fields would be:

              path-name i-number size uid

     The argument *n* in the *option* descriptions that follow is used as a
     decimal integer (optionally signed), where +*n* means more than *n*,
     −*n* means less than *n*, and *n* means exactly *n*. A day is defined
     as a 24 hour period.

     −I   Do not print the i-node number after each path
                 name.

     −l   Generate a supplementary list of all path names for
                 multiply linked files.

     −p *prefix*   The specified *prefix* will be added to each gen-
                 erated path name. The default is .

     −s   Print the file size, in bytes, after each path name.

     −u   Print the owner's login name after each path name.

     −a *n*   Select if the i-node has been accessed in *n* days.

     −m *n*   Select if the i-node has been modified in *n* days.

     −c *n*   Select if the i-node has been changed in *n* days.

     −n *file*   Select if the i-node has been modified more recently
                 than the argument *file*.

     −i *i-node-list* Generate names for only those i-nodes specified in
                 i-node-list.

EXAMPLES

To generate a list of the names of all files on a specified file system:

ff −I /dev/diskroot

To produce an index of files and i-numbers which are on a file system and have been modified in the last 24 hours:

ff −m −1 /dev/diskusr > /log/incbackup/usr/tuesday

To obtain the path names for i-nodes 451 and 76 on a specified file system:

ff −i 451,76 /dev/rdsk/0s7

SEE ALSO

finc(1M), find(1), frec(1M), ncheck(1M).

BUGS

Only a single path name out of any possible ones will be generated for a multiply linked i-node, unless the −l option is specified. When −l is specified, no selection criteria apply to the names generated. All possible names for every linked file on the file system will be included in the output.

On very large file systems, memory may run out before *ff* does.

NAME
:   filesave, tapesave — daily/weekly UNIX system file system backup

SYNOPSIS
:   **/etc/filesave.?**
    /etc/tapesave

DESCRIPTION
:   These shell scripts are provided as models. They are designed to provide a simple, interactive operator environment for file backup. *Filesave.?* is for daily disk-to-disk backup and *tapesave* is for weekly disk-to-tape.

    The suffix **.?** can be used to name another system where two (or more) machines share disk drives (or tape drives) and one or the other of the systems is used to perform backup on both.

SEE ALSO
:   shutdown(1M), volcopy(1M).

NAME
     finc — fast incremental backup

SYNOPSIS
     finc [selection-criteria] file-system raw-tape

DESCRIPTION
     Finc selectively copies the input *file-system* to the output *raw-tape*
     . The cautious will want to mount the input *file-system* read-only
     to insure an accurate backup, although acceptable results can be
     obtained in read-write mode. The tape must be previously labelled
     by *labelit* (see *volcopy*(1M)). The selection is controlled by the
     selection-criteria, accepting only those i-nodes/files for whom the
     conditions are true.

     It is recommended that production of a *finc* tape be preceded by
     the *ff* command, and the output of *ff* be saved as an index of the
     tape's contents. Files on a *finc* tape may be recovered with the
     frec command.

     The argument **n** in the *selection-criteria* which follow is used as a
     decimal integer (optionally signed), where $+n$ means more than n,
     $-n$ means less than n, and n means exactly n. A day is defined as
     a 24 hours.

     −**a** *n*   True if the file has been accessed in *n* days.

     −**m** *n*   True if the file has been modified in *n* days.

     −**c** *n*   True if the i-node has been changed in *n* days.

     −**n** *file*   True for any file which has been modified more
                       recently than the argument *file*.

EXAMPLES
     To write a tape consisting of all files from file-system **/usr** modified
     in the last 48 hours:

               finc −m −2 /dev/rdiskusr /dev/rmt/0m

SEE ALSO
     ff(1M), frec(1M), volcopy(1M).
     cpio(1) in the *UNIX Programmer's Manual—Volume 1: Com-
     mands and Utilities*.

NAME
>   frec − recover files from a backup tape

SYNOPSIS
>   /etc/frec [−p path] [−f reqfile] raw-tape i-number:name ...

DESCRIPTION
>   *Frec* recovers files from the specified *raw-tape* backup tape written
>   by *volcopy*(1M) or *finc*(1M), given their *i-numbers*. The data for
>   each recovery request will be written into the file given by *name*.
>
>   The −p option allows you to specify a default prefixing *path*
>   different from your current working directory. This will be
>   prefixed to any *names* that are not fully qualified, i.e., that do not
>   begin with / or ./. If any directories are missing in the paths of
>   recovery *names* they will be created.
>
>   −p *path*   Specifies a prefixing *path* to be used to fully
>   qualify any names that do not start with / or ./.
>
>   −f *reqfile*   Specifies a file which contains recovery requests.
>   The format is i-number:newname, one per line.

EXAMPLES
>   To recover a file, i-number 1216 when backed-up, into a file
>   named **junk** in your current working directory:
>
>   >   frec /dev/rmt/0m 1216:junk
>
>   To recover files with i-numbers 14156, 1232, and 3141 into files
>   **/usr/src/cmd/a**, **/usr/src/cmd/b** and **/usr/joe/a.c**:
>
>   >   frec −p /usr/src/cmd /dev/rmt/0m 14156:a 1232:b
>   >   3141:/usr/joe/a.c

SEE ALSO
>   ff(1M), finc(1M), volcopy(1M).
>   cpio(1) in the *UNIX Programmer's Manual—Volume 1: Com-*
>   *mands and Utilities*.

BUGS
>   While paving a path (i.e., creating the intermediate directories
>   contained in a path name) *frec* can only recover i-node fields for
>   those directories contained on the tape and requested for recovery.

NAME

fsck, dfsck — file system consistency check and interactive repair

SYNOPSIS

/etc/fsck [−y] [−n] [−sX] [−SX] [−t file] [−q] [−D] [−f]
[file-systems]

/etc/dfsck [options1] filsys1 ... − [options2] filsys2 ...

DESCRIPTION

Fsck

Fsck audits and interactively repairs inconsistent conditions for UNIX system files. If the file system is consistent then the number of files, number of blocks used, and number of blocks free are reported. If the file system is inconsistent the operator is prompted for concurrence before each correction is attempted. It should be noted that most corrective actions will result in some loss of data. The amount and severity of data lost may be determined from the diagnostic output. The default action for each consistency correction is to wait for the operator to respond **yes** or **no**. If the operator does not have write permission *fsck* will default to a −n action.

Fsck has more consistency checks than its predecessors *check*, *dcheck*, *fcheck*, and *icheck* combined.

The following options are interpreted by *fsck*.

−y   Assume a yes response to all questions asked by *fsck*.

−n   Assume a no response to all questions asked by *fsck*; do not open the file system for writing.

−sX Ignore the actual free list and (unconditionally) reconstruct a new one by rewriting the super-block of the file system. The file system should be unmounted while this is done; if this is not possible, care should be taken that the system is quiescent and that it is rebooted immediately afterwards. This precaution is necessary so that the old, bad, in-core copy of the superblock will not continue to be used, or written on the file system.

The −sX option allows for creating an optimal free-list organization. The following forms of X are supported for the following devices:

−s3 (RP03)
−s4 (RP04, RP05, RP06)
−sBlocks-per-cylinder:Blocks-to-skip (for anything else)

If *X* is not given, the values used when the file system was created are used. If these values were not specified, then the value *400:7* is used.

−S*X* Conditionally reconstruct the free list. This option is like −s*X* above except that the free list is rebuilt only if there were no discrepancies discovered in the file system. Using −S will force a no response to all questions asked by *fsck*. This option is useful for forcing free list reorganization on uncontaminated file systems.

−t If *fsck* cannot obtain enough memory to keep its tables, it uses a scratch file. If the −t option is specified, the file named in the next argument is used as the scratch file, if needed. Without the −t flag, *fsck* will prompt the operator for the name of the scratch file. The file chosen should not be on the file system being checked, and if it is not a special file or did not already exist, it is removed when *fsck* completes.

−q Quiet *fsck*. Do not print size-check messages in Phase 1. Unreferenced **fifos** will silently be removed. If *fsck* requires it, counts in the superblock will be automatically fixed and the free list salvaged.

−D Directories are checked for bad blocks. Useful after system crashes.

−f Fast check. Check block and sizes (Phase 1) and check the free list (Phase 5). The free list will be reconstructed (Phase 6) if it is necessary.

If no *file-systems* are specified, *fsck* will read a list of default file systems from the file **/etc/checklist**.

Inconsistencies checked are as follows:

1. Blocks claimed by more than one i-node or the free list.
2. Blocks claimed by an i-node or the free list outside the range of the file system.
3. Incorrect link counts.
4. Size checks:

Incorrect number of blocks.
Directory size not 16-byte aligned.
5.   Bad i-node format.
6.   Blocks not accounted for anywhere.
7.   Directory checks:
File pointing to unallocated i-node.
I-node number out of range.
8.   Super Block checks:
More than 65536 i-nodes.
More blocks for i-nodes than there are in
the file system.
9.   Bad free block list format.
10.   Total free block and/or free i-node count incorrect.

Orphaned files and directories (allocated but unreferenced) are, with the operator's concurrence, reconnected by placing them in the **lost +found** directory, if the files are nonempty. The user will be notified if the file or directory is empty or not. If it is empty, *fsck* will silently remove them. *Fsck* will force the reconnection of nonempty directories. The name assigned is the i-node number. The only restriction is that the directory **lost +found** must preexist in the root of the file system being checked and must have empty slots in which entries can be made. This is accomplished by making **lost +found**, copying a number of files to the directory, and then removing them (before *fsck* is executed).

Checking the raw device is almost always faster and should be used with everything but the *root* file system.

Dfsck

Dfsck allows two file system checks on two different drives simultaneously. *options1* and *options2* are used to pass options to *fsck* for the two sets of file systems. A − is the separator between the file system groups.

The *dfsck* program permits an operator to interact with two *fsck* (1M) programs at once. To aid in this, *dfsck* will print the file system name for each message to the operator. When answering a question from *dfsck*, the operator must prefix the response with a **1** or a **2** (indicating that the answer refers to the first or second file system group).

Do not use *dfsck* to check the *root* file system.

FILES

/etc/checklist   contains default list of file systems to
                      check.
/etc/checkall   optimizing *dfsck* shell file.

SEE ALSO

checkall(1M), clri(1M), ncheck(1M).
checklist(4), fs(4) in the *UNIX Programmer's Manual—Volume 2:
System Calls and Library Routines.*

BUGS

I-node numbers for . and .. in each directory should be checked
for validity.

DIAGNOSTICS

The diagnostics produced by *fsck* are intended to be self-
explanatory.

NAME
>   fsdb — file system debugger

SYNOPSIS
>   /etc/fsdb special [—]

DESCRIPTION

Fsdb can be used to patch up a damaged file system after a crash. It has conversions to translate block and i-numbers into their corresponding disk addresses. Also included are mnemonic offsets to access different parts of an i-node. These greatly simplify the process of correcting control block entries or descending the file system tree.

Fsdb contains several error-checking routines to verify i-node and block addresses. These can be disabled if necessary by invoking *fsdb* with the optional — argument or by the use of the **O** symbol. (*Fsdb* reads the i-size and f-size entries from the superblock of the file system as the basis for these checks.)

Numbers are considered decimal by default. Octal numbers must be prefixed with a zero. During any assignment operation, numbers are checked for a possible truncation error due to a size mismatch between source and destination.

Fsdb reads a block at a time and will therefore work with raw as well as block I/O. A buffer management routine is used to retain commonly used blocks of data in order to reduce the number of read system calls. All assignment operations result in an immediate write-through of the corresponding block.

The symbols recognized by *fsdb* are:

#	absolute address
i	convert from i-number to i-node address
b	convert to block address
d	directory slot offset
+,—	address arithmetic
q	quit
>,<	save, restore an address
=	numerical assignment
=+	incremental assignment
=—	decremental assignment
="	character string assignment
O	error checking flip flop
p	general print facilities

f	file print facility
B	byte mode
W	word mode
D	double word mode
!	escape to shell

The print facilities generate a formatted output in various styles. The current address is normalized to an appropriate boundary before printing begins. It advances with the printing and is left at the address of the last item printed. The output can be terminated at any time by typing the delete character. If a number follows the **p** symbol, that many entries are printed. A check is made to detect block boundary overflows since logically sequential blocks are generally not physically sequential. If a count of zero is used, all entries to the end of the current block are printed. The print options available are:

i	print as i-nodes
d	print as directories
o	print as octal words
e	print as decimal words
c	print as characters
b	print as octal bytes

The **f** symbol is used to print data blocks associated with the current i-node. If followed by a number, that block of the file is printed. (Blocks are numbered from zero.) The desired print option letter follows the block number, if present, or the **f** symbol. This print facility works for small as well as large files. It checks for special devices and that the block pointers used to find the data are not zero.

Dots, tabs, and spaces may be used as function delimiters but are not necessary. A line with just a new-line character will increment the current address by the size of the data type last printed. That is, the address is set to the next byte, word, double word, directory entry or i-node, allowing the user to step through a region of a file system. Information is printed in a format appropriate to the data type. Bytes, words and double words are displayed with the octal address followed by the value in octal and decimal. A **.B** or **.D** is appended to the address for byte and double word values, respectively. Directories are printed as a directory slot offset followed by the decimal i-number and the character representation of the entry name. I-nodes are printed with labeled fields describing each element.

The following mnemonics are used for i-node examination and refer to the current working i-node:

md	mode
ln	link count
uid	user ID number
gid	group ID number
sz	file size
a#	data block numbers (0 − 12)
at	access time
mt	modification time
maj	major device number
min	minor device number

EXAMPLES

386i	prints i-number 386 in an i-node format. This now becomes the current working i-node.
ln=4	changes the link count for the working i-node to 4.
ln=+1	increments the link count by 1.
fc	prints, in ASCII, block zero of the file associated with the working i-node.
2i.fd	prints the first 32 directory entries for the root i-node of this file system.
d5i.fc	changes the current i-node to that associated with the 5th directory entry (numbered from zero) found from the above command. The first logical block of the file is then printed in ASCII.
512B.p0o	prints the superblock of this file system in octal.
2i.a0b.d7=3	changes the i-number for the seventh directory slot in the root directory to 3. This example also shows how several operations can be combined on one command line.
d7.nm="name"	changes the name field in the directory slot to the given string. Quotes are optional when used with **nm** if the first character is alphabetic.
a2b.p0d	prints the third block of the current i-node as directory entries.

SEE ALSO
    fsck(1M).
    dir(4), fs(4) in the *UNIX Programmer's Manual—Volume 2: System Calls and Library Routines*.

NAME
     fuser — identify processes using a file or file structure

SYNOPSIS
     /etc/fuser [**−ku**] files [−] [[**−ku**] files]

DESCRIPTION
     Fuser lists the process IDs of the processes using the *files* specified
     as arguments. For block special devices, all processes using any
     file on that device are listed. The process ID is followed by **c, p** or
     r if the process is using the file as its current directory, the parent
     of its current directory (only when in use by the system), or its
     root directory, respectively. If the **−u** option is specified, the login
     name, in parentheses, also follows the process ID. In addition, if
     the **−k** option is specified, the SIGKILL signal is sent to each pro-
     cess. Only the super-user can terminate another user's process
     (see *kill*(2)). Options may be respecified between groups of files.
     The new set of options replaces the old set, with a lone dash can-
     celing any options currently in force.

     The process IDs are printed as a single line on the standard output,
     separated by spaces and terminated with a single new line. All
     other output is written on standard error.

EXAMPLES
     fuser −ku /dev/dsk/1s?
          will terminate all processes that are preventing disk drive
          one from being unmounted if typed by the super-user, list-
          ing the process ID and login name of each as it is killed.

     fuser −u /etc/passwd
          will list process IDs and login names of processes that have
          the password file open.

     fuser −ku /dev/dsk/1s? −u /etc/passwd
          will do both of the above examples in a single command
          line.

FILES
     /unix   for namelist
     /dev/kmem   for system image
     /dev/mem   also for system image

SEE ALSO

    mount(1M).

    ps(1) in the *UNIX Programmer's Manual—Volume 1: Commands and Utilities.*

    kill(2), signal(2) in the *UNIX Programmer's Manual—Volume 2: System Calls and Library Routines.*

NAME
    fwtmp, wtmpfix — manipulate connect accounting records

SYNOPSIS
    /usr/lib/acct/fwtmp [−ic]
    /usr/lib/acct/wtmpfix [files]

DESCRIPTION
    Fwtmp

    Fwtmp reads from the standard input and writes to the standard
    output, converting binary records of the type found in **wtmp** to for-
    matted ASCII records. The ASCII version is useful to enable edit-
    ing, via *ed*(1), bad records or general purpose maintenance of the
    file.

    The argument −**ic** is used to denote that input is in ASCII form,
    and output is to be written in binary form.

    Wtmpfix

    Wtmpfix examines the standard input or named files in **wtmp** for-
    mat, corrects the time/date stamps to make the entries consistent,
    and writes to the standard output. A − can be used in place of
    files to indicate the standard input. If time/date corrections are
    not performed, *acctcon1* will fault when it encounters certain
    date-change records.

    Each time the date is set, a pair of date change records are written
    to **/etc/wtmp**. The first record is the old date denoted by the
    string **old time** placed in the line field and the flag **OLD_TIME**
    placed in the type field of the **<utmp.h>** structure. The second
    record specifies the new date and is denoted by the string **new time**
    placed in the line field and the flag **NEW_TIME** placed in the type
    field. *Wtmpfix* uses these records to synchronize all time stamps
    in the file.

    In addition to correcting time/date stamps, *wtmpfix* will check the
    validity of the name field to ensure that it consists solely of
    alphanumeric characters or spaces. If it encounters a name that is
    considered invalid, it will change the login name to **INVALID** and
    write a diagnostic to the standard error. In this way, *wtmpfix*
    reduces the chance that *acctcon1* will fail when processing connect
    accounting records.

FILES
    /etc/wtmp
    /usr/include/utmp.h

SEE ALSO
      acct(1M),   acctcms(1M),   acctcon(1M),   acctmerg(1M),
      acctprc(1M), acctsh(1M), runacct(1M).
      acctcom(1), ed(1) in the *UNIX Programmer's Manual—Volume 1:*
      Commands and Utilities.
      acct(2), acct(4), utmp(4) in the *UNIX Programmer's Manual—*
      Volume 2: System Calls and Library Routines.

NAME
      getty — set terminal type, modes, speed, and line discipline
SYNOPSIS
      /etc/getty [−h] [−t timeout] line [speed [type [linedisc
      ]]]
      /etc/getty −c file

DESCRIPTION
      Getty is a program that is invoked by *init* (1M). It is the second
      process in the series, *(init-getty-login-shell)* that ultimately con-
      nects a user with the UNIX system. Initially *getty* prints the login
      message field for the entry it is using from **/etc/gettydefs**. *Getty*
      reads the user's login name and invokes the *login* (1) command
      with the user's name as argument. While reading the name, *getty*
      attempts to adapt the system to the speed and type of terminal
      being used.

      Line is the name of a tty line in **/dev** to which *getty* is to attach
      itself. *Getty* uses this string as the name of a file in the **/dev** direc-
      tory to open for reading and writing. Unless *getty* is invoked with
      the −h flag, *getty* will force a hangup on the line by setting the
      speed to zero before setting the speed to the default or specified
      speed. The −t flag plus *timeout* in seconds, specifies that *getty*
      should exit if the open on the line succeeds and no one types any-
      thing in the specified number of seconds. The optional second
      argument, *speed*, is a label to a speed and tty definition in the file
      /etc/gettydefs. This definition tells *getty* at what speed to initially
      run, what the login message should look like, what the initial tty
      settings are, and what speed to try next should the user indicate
      that the speed is inappropriate (by typing a *<break>* character).
      The default *speed* is 300 baud. The optional third argument, *type*,
      is a character string describing to *getty* what type of terminal is
      connected to the line in question. *Getty* understands the following
      types:

none	default
vt61	DEC vt61
vt100	DEC vt100
hp45	Hewlett-Packard 45
c100	Concept 100

      The default terminal is **none**; i.e., any crt or normal terminal unk-
      nown to the system. Also, for terminal type to have any meaning,
      the virtual terminal handlers must be compiled into the operating

system. They are available, but not compiled in the default condition. The optional fourth argument, *linedisc*, is a character string describing which line discipline to use in communicating with the terminal. Again the hooks for line disciplines are available in the operating system but there is only one presently available, the default line discipline, **LDISC0**.

When given no optional arguments, *getty* sets the *speed* of the interface to 300 baud, specifies that raw mode is to be used (awaken on every character), that echo is to be suppressed, either parity allowed, new-line characters will be converted to carriage return-line feed, and tab expansion performed on the standard output. It types the login message before reading the user's name a character at a time. If a null character (or framing error) is received, it is assumed to be the result of the user pushing the "break" key. This will cause *getty* to attempt the next *speed* in the series. The series that *getty* tries is determined by what it finds in **/etc/gettydefs**.

The user's name is terminated by a new-line or carriage-return character. The latter results in the system being set to treat carriage returns appropriately (see *ioctl* (2)).

The user's name is scanned to see if it contains any lower-case alphabetic characters; if not, and if the name is non-empty, the system is told to map any future upper-case characters into the corresponding lower-case characters.

Finally, *login* is called with the user's name as an argument. Additional arguments may be typed after the login name. These are passed to *login*, which will place them in the environment (see *login* (1)).

A check option is provided. When *getty* is invoked with the −**c** option and *file*, it scans the file as if it were scanning **/etc/gettydefs** and prints out the results to the standard output. If there are any unrecognized modes or improperly constructed entries, it reports these. If the entries are correct, it prints out the values of the various flags. See *ioctl* (2) to interpret the values. Note that some values are added to the flags automatically.

FILES

/etc/gettydefs
/etc/issue

SEE ALSO

init(1M), tty(7).

ct(1C), login(1) in the *UNIX Programmer's Manual—Volume 1: Commands and Utilities.*

ioctl(2), gettydefs(4), inittab(4) in the *UNIX Programmer's Manual—Volume 2: System Calls and Library Routines.*

BUGS

While *getty* does understand simple single character quoting conventions, it is not possible to quote the special control characters that *getty* uses to determine when the end of the line has been reached, which protocol is being used, and what the erase character is. Therefore it is not possible to login via *getty* and type a #, @, /, !, _, backspace, ^U, ^D, or & as part of your login name or arguments. They will always be interpreted as having their special meaning as described above.

NAME
   init, telinit — process control initialization

SYNOPSIS
   /etc/init [**0123456SsQq**]

   /etc/telinit [**0123456sSQqabc**]

DESCRIPTION
   Init

   Init is a general process spawner. Its primary role is to create
   processes from a script stored in the file **/etc/inittab** (see *inittab*(4)). This file usually has *init* spawn *getty*'s on each line that
   a user may log in on. It also controls autonomous processes
   required by any particular system.

   Init considers the system to be in a *run-level* at any given time. A
   run-level can be viewed as a software configuration of the system
   where each configuration allows only a selected group of processes
   to exist. The processes spawned by *init* for each of these *run-
   levels* is defined in the *inittab* file. *Init* can be in one of eight
   run-levels, **0 − 6** and **S** or **s**. The *run-level* is changed by having a
   privileged user run **/etc/init** (which is linked to *letc/telinit*). This
   user-spawned *init* sends appropriate signals to the orginal *init*
   spawned by the operating system when the system was rebooted,
   telling it which *run-level* to change to.

   Init is invoked inside the UNIX system as the last step in the boot
   procedure. The first thing *init* does is to look for **/etc/inittab** and
   see if there is an entry of the type *initdefault* (see *inittab*(4)). If
   there is, *init* uses the *run-level* specified in that entry as the initial
   run-level to enter. If this entry is not in *inittab* or *inittab* is not
   found, *init* requests that the user enter a *run-level* from the virtual
   system console, **/dev/syscon.** If an **S** (**s**) is entered, *init* goes into
   the *SINGLE USER* level. This is the only *run-level* that doesn't
   require the existence of a properly formatted *inittab* file. If
   /etc/inittab doesn't exist, then by default the only legal *run-level*
   that *init* can enter is the *SINGLE USER* level. In the *SINGLE
   USER* level the virtual console terminal **/dev/syscon** is opened for
   reading and writing and the command **/bin/su** is invoked immediately. To exit from the *SINGLE USER run-level* one of two
   options can be elected. First, if the shell is terminated (via an
   end-of-file), *init* will reprompt for a new *run-level*. Second, the
   init or *telinit* command can signal *init* and force it to change the
   run-level of the system.

When attempting to boot the system, failure of *init* to prompt for a
new *run-level* may be due to the fact that the device **/dev/syscon**
is linked to a device other than the physical system teletype
(**/dev/systty**). If this occurs, *init* can be forced to relink
/dev/syscon by typing a delete on the system teletype which is col-
located with the processor.

When *init* prompts for the new *run-level*, the operator may enter
only one of the digits **0** through **6** or the letters **S** or **s**. If **S** is
entered *init* operates as previously described in *SINGLE USER*
mode with the additional result that **/dev/syscon** is linked to the
user's terminal line, thus making it the virtual system console. A
message is generated on the physical console, **/dev/systty**, saying
where the virtual terminal has been relocated.

When *init* comes up initially and whenever it switches out of *SIN-
GLE USER* state to normal run states, it sets the *ioctl*(2) states of
the virtual console, **/dev/syscon**, to those modes saved in the file
/etc/ioctl.syscon. This file is written by *init* whenever *SINGLE
USER* mode is entered. If this file does not exist when *init* wants
to read it, a warning is printed and default settings are assumed.

If a **0** through **6** is entered *init* enters the corresponding *run-level*.
Any other input will be rejected and the user will be re-prompted.
If this is the first time *init* has entered a *run-level* other than *SIN-
GLE USER*, *init* first scans *inittab* for special entries of the type
boot and *bootwait*. These entries are performed, providing the
run-level entered matches that of the entry before any normal processing of *inittab* takes place. In this way any special initialization
of the operating system, such as mounting file systems, can take
place before users are allowed onto the system. The *inittab* file is
scanned to find all entries that are to be processed for that *run-
level*.

Run-level **2** is usually defined by the user to contain all of the terminal processes and daemons that are spawned in the multi-user
environment.

In a multi-user environment, the *inittab* file is usually set up so
that *init* will create a process for each terminal on the system.

For terminal processes, ultimately the shell will terminate because
of an end-of-file either typed explicitly or generated as the result of
hanging up. When *init* receives a child death signal, telling it that
a process it spawned has died, it records the fact and the reason it
died in **/etc/utmp** and **/etc/wtmp** if it exists (see *who*(1)). A

history of the processes spawned is kept in **/etc/wtmp** if such a file exists.

To spawn each process in the *inittab* file, *init* reads each entry and for each entry which should be respawned, it forks a child process. After it has spawned all of the processes specified by the *inittab* file, *init* waits for one of its descendant processes to die, a power-fail signal, or until *init* is signaled by *init* or *telinit* to change the system's *run-level*. When one of the above three conditions occurs, *init* re-examines the *inittab* file. New entries can be added to the *inittab* file at any time; however, *init* still waits for one of the above three conditions to occur. To provide for an instantaneous response the **init Q** or **init q** command can wake *init* to re-examine the *inittab* file.

If *init* receives a *powerfail* signal (*SIGPWR*) and is not in *SINGLE USER* mode, it scans *inittab* for special powerfail entries. These entries are invoked (if the *run-level*s permit) before any further processing takes place. In this way *init* can perform various cleanup and recording functions whenever the operating system experiences a power failure.

When *init* is requested to change *run-level*s (via *telinit*), *init* sends the warning signal (**SIGTERM**) to all processes that are undefined in the target *run-level*. *Init* waits 20 seconds before forcibly terminating these processes via the kill signal (**SIGKILL**).

Telinit

Telinit, which is linked to *letcfinit*, is used to direct the actions of *init*. It takes a one-character argument and signals *init* via the kill system call to perform the appropriate action. The following arguments serve as directives to *init*.

0−6	tells *init* to place the system in one of the *run-levels* **0−6**.
a,b,c	tells *init* to process only those **/etc/inittab** file entries having the **a, b** or **c** *run-level* set.
Q,q	tells *init* to re-examine the **/etc/inittab** file.
s,S	tells *init* to enter the single user environment. When this level change is effected, the virtual system teletype, **/dev/syscon**, is changed to the terminal from which the command was executed.

Telinit can only be run by someone who is super-user or a member of group **sys**.

FILES

/etc/inittab
/etc/utmp
/etc/wtmp
/etc/ioctl.syscon
/dev/syscon
/dev/systty

SEE ALSO

getty(1M).
login(1), sh(1), who(1) in the *UNIX Programmer's Manual — Volume 1: Commands and Utilities.*
kill(2), inittab(4), utmp(4) in the *UNIX Programmer's Manual — Volume 2: System Calls and Library Routines.*

DIAGNOSTICS

If *init* finds that it is continuously respawning an entry from **/etc/inittab** more than 10 times in 2 minutes, it will assume that there is an error in the command string, and generate an error message on the system console, and refuse to respawn this entry until either 5 minutes has elapsed or it receives a signal from a user *init* (*telinit*). This prevents *init* from eating up system resources when someone makes a typographical error in the *inittab* file or a program is removed that is referenced in the *inittab*.

NAME
   install − install commands

SYNOPSIS
   /etc/install [−**c** dira] [−**f** dirb] [−**i**] [−**n** dirc] [−**o**] [−**s**] file
   [dirx ...]

DESCRIPTION
   Install is a command most commonly used in "makefiles" (see
   make(1)) to install a *file* (updated target file) in a specific place
   within a file system. Each *file* is installed by copying it into the
   appropriate directory, thereby retaining the mode and owner of the
   original command. The program prints messages telling the user
   exactly what files it is replacing or creating and where they are
   going.

   If no options or directories (*dirx* ...) are given, *install* will search
   a set of default directories (**/bin, /usr/bin, /etc, /lib**, and **/usr/lib**,
   in that order) for a file with the same name as *file*. When the first
   occurrence is found, *install* issues a message saying that it is
   overwriting that file with *file*, and proceeds to do so. If the file is
   not found, the program states this and exits without further action.

   If one or more directories (*dirx* ...) are specified after *file*, those
   directories will be searched before the directories specified in the
   default list.

   The meanings of the options are:

   −**c** *dira*   Installs a new command (*file*) in the direc-
                    tory specified by *dira*, only if it is not
                    found. If it is found, *install* issues a mes-
                    sage saying that the file already exists, and
                    exits without overwriting it. May be used
                    alone or with the −**s** option.

   −**f** *dirb*   Forces *file* to be installed in given direc-
                    tory, whether or not one already exists. If
                    the file being installed does not already
                    exist, the mode and owner of the new file
                    will be set to **755** and **bin**, respectively. If
                    the file already exists, the mode and owner
                    will be that of the already existing file.
                    May be used alone or with the −**o** or −**s**
                    options.

−i	Ignores default directory list, searching only through the given directories (*dirx ...*). May be used alone or with any other options other than −c and −f.
−n *dirc*	If *file* is not found in any of the searched directories, it is put in the directory specified in *dirc*. The mode and owner of the new file will be set to 755 and bin, respectively. May be used alone or with any other options other than −c and −f.
−o	If *file* is found, this option saves the "found" file by copying it to OLD*file* in the directory in which it was found. This option is useful when installing a normally text busy file such as /bin/sh or /etc/getty, where the existing file cannot be removed. May be used alone or with any other options other than −c.
−s	Suppresses printing of messages other than error messages. May be used alone or with any other options.

SEE ALSO

mk(8).

make(1) in the *UNIX Programmer's Manual—Volume 1: Commands and Utilities.*

NAME
     killall — kill all active processes

SYNOPSIS
     /etc/killall [signal]

DESCRIPTION
     Killall is a procedure used by **/etc/shutdown** to kill all active
     processes not directly related to the shutdown procedure.

     Killall is chiefly used to terminate all processes with open files so
     that the mounted file systems will be unbusied and can be
     unmounted.

     Killall sends *signal* (see *kill*(1)) to all remaining processes not
     belonging to the above group of exclusions. If no *signal* is
     specified, a default of **9** is used.

FILES
     /etc/shutdown

SEE ALSO
     fuser(1M), shutdown(1M).
     kill(1), ps(1) in the *UNIX Programmer's Manual—Volume 1:
     Commands and Utilities.*
     signal(2) in the *UNIX Programmer's Manual—Volume 2: System
     Calls and Library Routines.*

NAME
>   link, unlink — exercise link and unlink system calls

SYNOPSIS
>   **/etc/link** file1 file2
>   **/etc/unlink** file

DESCRIPTION
>   *Link* and *unlink* perform their respective system calls on their
>   arguments, abandoning all error checking. These commands may
>   only be executed by the super-user, who (it is hoped) knows what
>   he or she is doing.

SEE ALSO
>   rm(1) in the *UNIX Programmer's Manual—Volume 1: Com-
>   mands and Utilities.*
>   link(2), unlink(2) in the *UNIX Programmer's Manual—Volume 2:
>   System Calls and Library Routines.*

NAME
> lpadmin — configure the LP spooling system

SYNOPSIS
> /usr/lib/lpadmin −p printer [options]
> /usr/lib/lpadmin −x dest
> /usr/lib/lpadmin −d[dest]

DESCRIPTION
> *Lpadmin* configures LP spooling systems to describe printers, classes and devices. It is used to add and remove destinations, change membership in classes, change devices for printers, change printer interface programs and to change the system default destination. *Lpadmin* may not be used when the LP scheduler, *lpsched* (1M), is running, except where noted below.
>
> Exactly one of the −p, −d or −x options must be present for every legal invocation of *lpadmin*.

> −d[*dest*]   makes *dest*, an existing destination, the new system default destination. If *dest* is not supplied, then there is no system default destination. This option may be used when *lpsched* (1M) is running. No other *options* are allowed with −d.

> −x*dest*   removes destination *dest* from the LP system. If *dest* is a printer and is the only member of a class, then the class will be deleted, too. No other *options* are allowed with −x.

> −p*printer*   names a *printer* to which all of the *options* below refer. If *printer* does not exist then it will be created.

> The following *options* are only useful with −p and may appear in any order. For ease of discussion, the printer will be referred to as *P* below.

> −c*class*   inserts printer *P* into the specified *class*. *Class* will be created if it does not already exist.

> −e*printer*   copies an existing *printer's* interface program to be the new interface program for *P*.

> −h   indicates that the device associated with *P* is hardwired. This *option* is assumed when creating a new printer unless the −l *option* is supplied.

−i*interface*   establishes a new interface program for *P*. *Interface* is the path name of the new program.

−l   indicates that the device associated with *P* is a login terminal. The LP scheduler, *lpsched*(1M), disables all login terminals automatically each time it is started. Before re-enabling *P*, its current *device* should be established using *lpadmin*.

−m*model*   selects a model interface program for *P*. *Model* is one of the model interface names supplied with the LP software (see *Models* below).

−r*class*   removes printer *P* from the specified *class*. If *P* is the last member of the *class*, then the *class* will be removed.

−v*device*   associates a new *device* with printer *P*. *Device* is the path name of a file that is writable by the LP administrator, *lp*. Note that there is nothing to stop an administrator from associating the same *device* with more than one *printer*. If only the −p and −v *options* are supplied, then *lpadmin* may be used while the scheduler is running.

Restrictions.
When creating a new printer, the −v option and one of the −e, −i or −m options must be supplied. Only one of the −e, −i or −m options may be supplied. The −h and −l keyletters are mutually exclusive. Printer and class names may be no longer than 14 characters and must consist entirely of the characters **A-Z**, **a-z**, **0-9** and _ (underscore).

Models.
Model printer interface programs are supplied with the LP software. They are shell procedures which interface between *lpsched (1M)* and devices. All models reside in the directory **/usr/spool/lp/model** and may be used as is with *lpadmin* −m. Models should have 644 permission if owned by lp & bin, or 664 permission if owned by bin & bin. Alternatively, LP administrators may modify copies of models and then use *lpadmin* −i to associate them with printers. The following list describes the *models* and lists the options which they may be given on the *lp* command line using the −o keyletter:

dumb   interface for a line printer without special functions and protocol. Form feeds are assumed. This is a good model to copy and modify for printers which do not have models.

1640   DIABLO 1640 terminal running at 1200 baud, using XON/XOFF protocol. Options:

-   **−12**   12-pitch (10-pitch is the default)
-   **−f**   do not use the *450*(1) filter. The output has been pre-processed by either *450*(1) or the *nroff (1)* 450 driving table.

hp   Hewlett-Packard 2631A line printer at 2400 baud. Options:

-   **−c**   compressed print
-   **−e**   expanded print

prx   Printronix P300 or P600 printer using XON/XOFF protocol at 1200 baud.

EXAMPLES

1. Assuming there is an existing Hewlett-Packard 2631A line printer named *hp2*, it will use the **hp** model interface after the command:

    /usr/lib/lpadmin −php2 −mhp

2. To obtain compressed print on *hp2*, use the command:

    lp −dhp2 −o−c files

3. A DIABLO 1640 printer called *st1* can be added to the LP configuration with the command:

    /usr/lib/lpadmin −pst1 −v/dev/tty20 −m1640

4. An *nroff (1)* document may be printed on *st1* in any of the following ways:

    nroff −T450 files | lp −dst1 −of
    nroff −T450−12 files | lp −dst1 −of
    nroff −T37 files | col | lp −dst1

5. The following command prints the password file on *st1* in 12-pitch:

    lp −dst1 −o12 /etc/passwd

NOTE: the **−12** option to the **1640** model should never be used in conjunction with *nroff*(1).

FILES

/usr/spool/lp/*

SEE ALSO

accept(1M), lpsched(1M).

enable(1), lp(1), lpstat(1), nroff(1) in the *UNIX Programmer's Manual—Volume 1: Commands and Utilities.*

NAME
>   lpsched, lpshut, lpmove — start/stop the LP request scheduler and
>   move requests

SYNOPSIS
>   **/usr/lib/lpsched**
>   **/usr/lib/lpshut**
>   **/usr/lib/lpmove** requests dest
>   **/usr/lib/lpmove** dest1   dest2

DESCRIPTION
>   *Lpsched* schedules requests taken by *lp*(1) for printing on line
>   printers.
>
>   *Lpshut* shuts down the line printer scheduler. All printers that are
>   printing at the time *lpshut* is invoked will stop printing. Requests
>   that were printing at the time a printer was shut down will be
>   reprinted in their entirety after *lpsched* is started again. All LP
>   commands perform their functions even when *lpsched* is not run-
>   ning.
>
>   *Lpmove* moves requests that were queued by *lp*(1) between LP
>   destinations. This command may be used only when *lpsched* is not
>   running.
>
>   The first form of the command moves the named *requests* to the
>   LP destination, *dest*. *Requests* are request ids as returned by
>   *lp*(1). The second form moves all requests for destination *dest1* to
>   destination *dest2*. As a side effect, *lp* *(1)* will reject requests for
>   *dest1*.
>
>   Note that *lpmove* never checks the acceptance status (see
>   *accept*(1M)) for the new destination when moving requests.

FILES
>   /usr/spool/lp/*

SEE ALSO
>   accept(1M), lpadmin(1M).
>   enable(1), lp(1), lpstat(1) in the *UNIX Programmer's Manual —*
>   *Volume 1: Commands and Utilities.*

NAME

mkfs — construct a file system

SYNOPSIS

/etc/mkfs special blocks[:i-nodes] [gap blocks/cyl]

/etc/mkfs special proto [gap blocks/cyl]

DESCRIPTION

Mkfs constructs a file system by writing on the special file according to the directions found in the remainder of the command line. The command waits 10 seconds before starting to construct the file system. If the second argument is given as a string of digits, *mkfs* builds a file system with a single empty directory on it. The size of the file system is the value of *blocks* interpreted as a decimal number. This is the number of *physical* disk blocks the file system will occupy. The boot program is left uninitialized. If the optional number of i-nodes is not given, the default is the number of *logical* blocks divided by 4.

If the second argument is a file name that can be opened, *mkfs* assumes it to be a prototype file *proto*, and will take its directions from that file. The prototype file contains tokens separated by spaces or new-lines. The first token is the name of a file to be copied onto block zero as the bootstrap program. The second token is a number specifying the size of the created file system in *physical* disk blocks. Typically it will be the number of blocks on the device, perhaps diminished by space for swapping. The next token is the number of i-nodes in the file system. The maximum number of i-nodes configurable is 65500. The next set of tokens comprise the specification for the root file. File specifications consist of tokens giving the mode, the user ID, the group ID, and the initial contents of the file. The syntax of the contents field depends on the mode.

The mode token for a file is a 6-character string. The first character specifies the type of the file. (The characters **−bcd** specify regular, block special, character special and directory files respectively.) The second character of the type is either **u** or **−** to specify set-user-id mode or not. The third is **g** or **−** for the set-group-id mode. The rest of the mode is a 3 digit octal number giving the owner, group, and other read, write, execute permissions (see *chmod*(1)).

Two decimal number tokens come after the mode; they specify the user and group IDs of the owner of the file.

If the file is a regular file, the next token is a path name whence the contents and size are copied. If the file is a block or character special file, two decimal number tokens follow which give the major and minor device numbers. If the file is a directory, *mkfs* makes the entries . and .. and then reads a list of names and (recursively) files specifications for the entries in the directory. The scan is terminated with the token **$**.

A sample prototype specification follows:

```
/stand/diskboot
4872 110
d——777 3 1
usr      d——777 3 1
  sh       ———755 3 1 /bin/sh
  ken      d——755 6 1
           $
  b0       b——644 3 1 0 0
  c0       c——644 3 1 0 0
           $
       $
```

In both command syntaxes, the rotational *gap* and the number of *blocks/cyl* can be specified. The following values are recommended:

Device	Gap Size	Blks/Cyl
RL01/02	7	40
RP03	5	200
RP04/05/06	7	418
RP07	7	400
RM03	7	160
RM05	7	608
RM80	9	434
3B20 computer MHD	7	608
default	7	400

The *default* will be used if the supplied *gap* and *blocks/cyl* are considered illegal values or if a short argument count occurs.

SEE ALSO

    chmod(1) in the *UNIX Programmer's Manual — Volume 1: Commands and Utilities.*

    dir(4), fs(4) in the *UNIX Programmer's Manual — Volume 2: System Calls and Library Routines.*

BUGS

    If a prototype is used, it is not possible to initialize a file larger than 64K bytes, nor is there a way to specify links.

NAME
     mknod — build special file

SYNOPSIS
     /etc/mknod name **c** | **b** major minor
     /etc/mknod name **p**

DESCRIPTION
     Mknod makes a directory entry and corresponding i-node for a
     special file. The first argument is the *name* of the entry. In the
     first case, the second is **b** if the special file is block-type (disks,
     tape) or **c** if it is character-type (other devices). The last two
     arguments are numbers specifying the *major* device type and the
     minor device (e.g., unit, drive, or line number), which may be
     either decimal or octal.

     The assignment of major device numbers is specific to each system.
     They have to be dug out of the system source file **conf.c**.

     Mknod can also be used to create fifo's (a.k.a named pipes)
     (second case in *SYNOPSIS* above).

SEE ALSO
     mknod(2) in the *UNIX Programmer's Manual—Volume 2: Sys-
     tem Calls and Library Routines.*

NAME
    mount, umount — mount and dismount file system

SYNOPSIS
    /etc/mount [special directory [**−r**]]

    /etc/umount special

DESCRIPTION
    Mount announces to the system that a removable file system is
    present on the device *special*. The *directory* must exist already; it
    becomes the name of the root of the newly mounted file system.

    These commands maintain a table of mounted devices. If invoked
    with no arguments, *mount* prints the table.

    The optional last argument indicates that the file is to be mounted
    read-only. Physically write-protected and magnetic tape file sys-
    tems must be mounted in this way or errors will occur when access
    times are updated, whether or not any explicit write is attempted.

    Umount announces to the system that the removable file system
    previously mounted on device *special* is to be removed.

FILES
    /etc/mnttab   mount table

SEE ALSO
    setmnt(1M).
    mount(2), mnttab(4) in the *UNIX Programmer's Manual —
    Volume 2: System Calls and Library Routines*.

DIAGNOSTICS
    Mount issues a warning if the file system to be mounted is
    currently mounted under another name.

    Umount complains if the special file is not mounted or if it is busy.
    The file system is busy if it contains an open file or some user's
    working directory.

BUGS
    Some degree of validation is done on the file system; however, it is
    generally unwise to mount garbage file systems.

NAME
     mvdir — move a directory

SYNOPSIS
     /etc/mvdir dirname   name

DESCRIPTION
     Mvdir moves directories within a file system. *Dirname* must be a
     directory; *name* must not exist. Neither name may be a sub-set of
     the other (**/x/y** cannot be moved to **/x/y/z**, nor vice versa).

     Only super-user can use *mvdir*.

SEE ALSO
     mkdir(1) in the *UNIX Programmer's Manual—Volume 1: Com-
     mands and Utilities.*

NAME
      ncheck — generate names from i-numbers

SYNOPSIS
      /etc/ncheck [−i numbers] [−a] [−s] [file-system]

DESCRIPTION
      Ncheck with no argument generates a path-name vs. i-number list
      of all files on a set of default file systems. Names of directory files
      are followed by /.. The −i option reduces the report to only those
      files whose i-numbers follow. The −a option allows printing of the
      names . and .., which are ordinarily suppressed. The −s option
      reduces the report to special files and files with set-user-ID mode;
      it is intended to discover concealed violations of security policy.

      A file system may be specified.

      The report is in no useful order, and probably should be sorted.

SEE ALSO
      fsck(1M).
      sort(1) in the *UNIX Programmer's Manual — Volume 1: Com-*
      mands and Utilities.

DIAGNOSTICS
      When the file system structure is improper, ?? denotes the
      "parent" of a parentless file and a path-name beginning with ...
      denotes a loop.

NAME
>   prfld, prfstat, prfdc, prfsnap, prfpr — operating system profiler

SYNOPSIS
>   **/etc/prfld** [namelist]
>   **/etc/prfstat on**
>   **/etc/prfstat off**
>   **/etc/prfdc** file [period [off_hour]]
>   **/etc/prfsnap** file
>   **/etc/prfpr** file [cutoff [namelist]]

DESCRIPTION
>   *Prfld*, *prfstat*, *prfdc*, *prfsnap*, and *prfpr* form a system of pro-
>   grams to facilitate an activity study of the UNIX operating system.
>
>   *Prfld* is used to initialize the recording mechanism in the system.
>   It generates a table containing the starting address of each system
>   subroutine as extracted from *namelist*.
>
>   *Prfstat* is used to enable or disable the sampling mechanism.
>   Profiler overhead is less than 1% as calculated for 500 text
>   addresses. *Prfstat* will also reveal the number of text addresses
>   being measured.
>
>   *Prfdc* and *prfsnap* perform the data collection function of the
>   profiler by copying the current value of all the text address
>   counters to a file where the data can be analyzed. *Prfdc* will store
>   the counters into *file* every *period* minutes and will turn off at
>   *off_hour* (valid values for *off_hour* are **0−24**). *Prfsnap* collects
>   data at the time of invocation only, appending the counter values
>   to *file*.
>
>   *Prfpr* formats the data collected by *prfdc* or *prfsnap*. Each text
>   address is converted to the nearest text symbol (as found in *namel-
>   ist*) and is printed if the percent activity for that range is greater
>   than *cutoff*.

FILES
>   /dev/prf   interface to profile data and text addresses
>   /unix   default for namelist file

SEE ALSO
>   prf(7).

NAME
     pwck, grpck — password/group file checkers

SYNOPSIS
     /etc/pwck [file]
     /etc/grpck [file]

DESCRIPTION
     Pwck scans the password file and notes any inconsistencies. The
     checks include validation of the number of fields, login name, user
     ID, group ID, and whether the login directory and optional pro-
     gram name exist. The default password file is **/etc/passwd**.

     Grpck verifies all entries in the group file. This verification
     includes a check of the number of fields, group name, group ID,
     and whether all login names appear in the password file. The
     default group file is **/etc/group**.

FILES
     /etc/group
     /etc/passwd

SEE ALSO
     group(4), passwd(4) in the *UNIX Programmer's Manual —
     Volume 2: System Calls and Library Routines.*

DIAGNOSTICS
     Group entries in **/etc/group** with no login names are flagged.

NAME
     runacct — run daily accounting
SYNOPSIS
     /usr/lib/acct/runacct [mmdd [state]]
DESCRIPTION
     Runacct is the main daily accounting shell procedure. It is nor-
     mally initiated via *cron*(1M). *Runacct* processes connect, fee,
     disk, and process accounting files. It also prepares summary files
     for *prdaily* or billing purposes.

     Runacct takes care not to damage active accounting files or sum-
     mary files in the event of errors. It records its progress by writing
     descriptive diagnostic messages into **active**. When an error is
     detected, a message is written to **/dev/console**, mail (see *mail*(1))
     is sent to **root** and **adm**, and *runacct* terminates. *Runacct* uses a
     series of lock files to protect against re-invocation. The files **lock**
     and **lock1** are used to prevent simultaneous invocation, and **last-
     date** is used to prevent more than one invocation per day.

     Runacct breaks its processing into separate, restartable *states*
     using **statefile** to remember the last *state* completed. It accom-
     plishes this by writing the *state* name into **statefile**. *Runacct* then
     looks in **statefile** to see what it has done and to determine what to
     process next. *States* are executed in the following order:

SETUP	Move active accounting files into working files.
WTMPFIX	Verify integrity of **wtmp** file, correcting date changes if necessary.
CONNECT1	Produce connect session records in **ctmp.h** format.
CONNECT2	Convert **ctmp.h** records into **tacct.h** format.
PROCESS	Convert process accounting records into **tacct.h** format.
MERGE	Merge the connect and process account-ing records.
FEES	Convert output of *chargefee* into **tacct.h** format and merge with connect and pro-cess accounting records.

DISK	Merge disk accounting records with connect, process, and fee accounting records.
MERGETACCT	Merge the daily total accounting records in **daytacct** with the summary total accounting records in **/usr/adm/acct/sum/tacct**.
CMS	Produce command summaries.
USEREXIT	Any installation-dependent accounting programs can be included here.
CLEANUP	Cleanup temporary files and exit.

To restart *runacct* after a failure, first check the **active** file for diagnostics, then fix up any corrupted data files such as **pacct** or **wtmp**. The **lock** files and **lastdate** file must be removed before *runacct* can be restarted. The argument *mmdd* is necessary if *runacct* is being restarted, and specifies the month and day for which *runacct* will rerun the accounting. Entry point for processing is based on the contents of **statefile**; to override this, include the desired *state* on the command line to designate where processing should begin.

EXAMPLES

To start *runacct*.

    nohup runacct 2> /usr/adm/acct/nite/fd2log &

To restart *runacct*.

    nohup runacct 0601 2>> /usr/adm/acct/nite/fd2log &

To restart *runacct* at a specific *state*.

    nohup   runacct   0601   MERGE   2>>
    /usr/adm/acct/nite/fd2log &

FILES

    /etc/wtmp
    /usr/adm/pacct*
    /usr/src/cmd/acct/tacct.h
    /usr/src/cmd/acct/ctmp.h
    /usr/adm/acct/nite/active
    /usr/adm/acct/nite/daytacct
    /usr/adm/acct/nite/lock
    /usr/adm/acct/nite/lock1
    /usr/adm/acct/nite/lastdate
    /usr/adm/acct/nite/statefile
    /usr/adm/acct/nite/ptacct*.*mmdd*

SEE ALSO

acct(1M),   acctcms(1M),   acctcon(1M),   acctmerg(1M),
acctprc(1M), acctsh(1M), cron(1M), fwtmp(1M).
acctcom(1), mail(1) in the *UNIX Programmer's Manual —
Volume 1: Commands and Utilities.*
acct(2), acct(4), utmp(4) in the *UNIX Programmer's Manual —
Volume 2: System Calls and Library Routines.*

BUGS

Normally it is not a good idea to restart *runacct* in the **SETUP**
state. Run **SETUP** manually and restart via:

runacct *mmdd* **WTMPFIX**

If *runacct* failed in the **PROCESS** *state,* remove the last **ptacct** file
because it will not be complete.

NAME
     sadp — disk access profiler

SYNOPSIS
     sadp [**−th**] [**−d** device[−drive]] s [n]

DESCRIPTION
     Sadp reports disk access location and seek distance, in tabular or
     histogram form. It samples disk activity once every second during
     an interval of *s* seconds. This is done repeatedly if *n* is specified.
     Cylinder usage and disk distance are recorded in units of 8
     cylinders.

     Valid values of *device* are **rp06, rm05,** and **disk.** *Drive* specifies
     the disk drives and it may be:

          a drive number in the range supported by *device*,
          two numbers separated by a minus (indicating an inclusive
          range),
     or
          a list of drive numbers separated by commas.

     Up to 8 disk drives may be reported. The −**d** option may be omit-
     ted, if only one *device* is present.

     The −**t** flag causes the data to be reported in tabular form. The
     −**h** flag produces a histogram on the printer of the data. Default
     is −**t**.

EXAMPLE
     The command:

               sadp −d rp06 −0 900 4

     will generate 4 tabular reports, each describing cylinder usage and
     seek distance of rp06 disk drive 0 during a 15-minute interval.

FILES
     /dev/kmem

NAME
     sa1, sa2, sadc — system activity report package
SYNOPSIS
     /usr/lib/sa/sadc [t n] [ofile]

     /usr/lib/sa/sa1 [t n]

     /usr/lib/sa/sa2 [−ubdycwaqvwprA] [−s time] [−e time] [−i sec]
DESCRIPTION
     System activity data can be accessed at the special request of a
     user [see *sar*(1)] and automatically on a routine basis as described
     here. The operating system contains a number of counters that
     are incremented as various system actions occur. These include
     CPU utilization counters, buffer usage counters, disk and tape I/O
     activity counters, TTY device activity counters, switching and
     system-call counters, file-access counters, queue activity counters,
     and counters for interprocess communications.

     Sadc and shell procedures, *sa1* and *sa2*, are used to sample, save,
     and process this data.

     Sadc, the data collector, samples system data *n* times every *t*
     seconds and writes in binary format to *ofile* or to standard output.
     If *t* and *n* are omitted, a special record is written. This facility is
     used at system boot time to mark the time at which the counters
     restart from zero. The **/etc/rc** entry:

          su sys −c "/usr/lib/sa/sadc /usr/adm/sa/sa'date +%d'"

     writes the special record to the daily data file to mark the system
     restart.

     The shell script *sa1*, a variant of *sadc*, is used to collect and store
     data in binary file **/usr/adm/sa/sa**dd where *dd* is the current day.
     The arguments *t* and *n* cause records to be written *n* times at an
     interval of *t* seconds, or once if omitted. The
     /usr/spool/cron/crontabs/sys entries [see *cron*(1M)]:

          0 * * * 0,6 /usr/lib/sa/sa1
          0 8−17 * * 1−5 /usr/lib/sa/sa1 1200 3
          0 18−7 * * 1−5 /usr/lib/sa/sa1

will produce records every 20 minutes during working hours and hourly otherwise.

The shell script *sa2*, a variant of *sar*(1), writes a daily report in file **/usr/adm/sa/sar**dd. The options are explained in *sar*(1). The **/usr/spool/cron/crontabs/sys** entry:

5 18 * * 1—5 /usr/lib/sa/sa2 —s 8:00 —e 18:01 —i 3600 —A

will report important activities hourly during the working day.

The structure of the binary daily data file is:

```
struct sa {
        struct sysinfo si;      /* see /usr/include/sys/sysinfo.h */
        struct minfo mi;        /* defined in /usr/include/sys/sysinfo.h */
        int  szinode;           /* current size of inode table */
        int  szfile;            /* current size of file table */
        int  szproc;            /* current size of proc table */
        int  szlckf;            /* current size of file record header table */
        int  szlckr;            /* current size of file record lock table */
        int  mszinode;          /* size of inode table */
        int  mszfile;           /* size of file table */
        int  mszproc;           /* size of proc table */
        int  mszlckf;         /* maximum size of file record header table */
        int  mszlckr;           /* maximum size of file record lock table */
        long  inodeovf;         /* cumulative overflows of inode table */
        long  fileovf;          /* cumulative overflows of file table */
        long  procovf;          /* cumulative overflows of proc table */
        time_t  ts;             /* time stamp */
        int  apstate;
        long  devio[NDEVS][4];          /* device unit information */
#define IO_OPS          0       /* cumulative I/O requests */
#define IO_BCNT         1       /* cumulative blocks transferred */
#define IO_ACT          2       /* cumulative drive busy time in ticks */
#define IO_RESP         3       /* cumul. I/O resp time in ticks since boot */
};
```

FILES

/usr/adm/sa/sa*dd*	daily data file
/usr/adm/sa/sar*dd*	daily report file
/tmp/sa.adrfl	address file

SEE ALSO
>   cron(1M).
>   sag(1G), sar(1), timex(1) in the *UNIX Programmer's Manual —
>   Volume 1: Commands and Utilities.*

NAME
     setmnt — establish mount table
SYNOPSIS
     /etc/setmnt
DESCRIPTION
     Setmnt creates the **/etc/mnttab** table (see *mnttab*(4)), which is
     needed for both the *mount*(1M) and *umount* commands. *Setmnt*
     reads standard input and creates a *mnttab* entry for each line.
     Input lines have the format:

          filesys node

     where *filesys* is the name of the file system's *special file* (e.g.,
     "dsk/?s?") and *node* is the root name of that file system. Thus
     filesys and *node* become the first two strings in the *mnttab*(4)
     entry.

FILES
     /etc/mnttab

SEE ALSO
     mount(1M).
     mnttab(4) in the *UNIX Programmer's Manual — Volume 2: Sys-
     tem Calls and Library Routines.*

BUGS
     Evil things will happen if *filesys* or *node* are longer than 32 char-
     acters.
     Setmnt silently enforces an upper limit on the maximum number
     of *mnttab* entries.

NAME

shutdown — terminate all processing

SYNOPSIS

/etc/shutdown

DESCRIPTION

Shutdown is part of the UNIX system operation procedures. Its primary function is to terminate all currently running processes in an orderly and cautious manner. The procedure is designed to interact with the operator (i.e., the person who invoked *shutdown*). *Shutdown* may instruct the operator to perform some specific tasks, or to supply certain responses before execution can resume. *Shutdown* goes through the following steps:

All users logged on the system are notified to log off the system by a broadcasted message. The operator may display his/her own message at this time. Otherwise, the standard file-save message is displayed.

If the operator wishes to run the file-save procedure, *shutdown* unmounts all file systems.

All file systems' super blocks are updated before the system is to be stopped (see *sync*(1)). This must be done before re-booting the system, to insure file system integrity. The most common error diagnostic that will occur is *device busy*. This diagnostic happens when a particular file system could not be unmounted.

SEE ALSO

mount(1M).
sync(1) in the *UNIX Programmer's Manual—Volume 1: Commands and Utilities*.

NAME

swap — swap administrative interface

SYNOPSIS

/etc/swap −a swapdev swaplow swaplen

/etc/swap −d swapdev swaplow

/etc/swap −l

DESCRIPTION

Swap provides a method of adding, deleting, and monitoring the system swap areas used by the memory manager. The following options are recognized:

−a Add the specified swap area. *Swapdev* is the name of block special device, e.g., **/dev/dsk/1s0**. *Swaplow* is the offset in 512-byte blocks into the device where the swap area should begin. *Swaplen* is the length of the swap area in 512-byte blocks. This option can only be used by the super-user. Swap areas are normally added by the system start-up routine **/etc/rc** when going into multiuser mode.

−d Delete the specified swap area. *Swapdev* is the name of block special device, e.g., **/dev/dsk/1s0**. *Swaplow* is the offset in 512-byte blocks into the device where the swap area should begin. Using this option marks the swap area as "being deleted." The system will not allocate any new blocks from the area, and will try to free swap blocks from it. The area will remain in use until all blocks from it are freed. This option can only be used by the super-user.

−l List the status of all the swap areas. The output has four columns:

   DEV   The *swapdev* special file for the swap area if one can be found in the **/dev/dsk** or **/dev** directories, and its major/minor device number in decimal.

   LOW   The *swaplow* value for the area in 512-byte blocks.

   LEN   The *swaplen* value for the area in 512-byte blocks.

   FREE The number of free 512-byte blocks in the area. If the swap area is being deleted, this column will be marked (**indel**).

WARNINGS

No check is done to see if a swap area being added overlaps with an existing swap area or file system.

98−System Administration Facilities   UNIX Programmer's Manual

NAME
sysdef — system definition

SYNOPSIS
/etc/sysdef [opsys [master]]

DESCRIPTION
Sysdef analyzes the named operating system file and extracts configuration information. This includes all hardware devices as well as system devices and all tunable parameters.

The output of *sysdef* can usually be used directly by *config*(1M) to regenerate the appropriate configuration files.

FILES
/unix   default operating system file
/etc/master   default table for hardware specifications

SEE ALSO
config(1M).
master(4) in the *UNIX Programmer's Manual—Volume 2: System Calls and Library Routines.*

BUGS
For devices that have interrupt vectors but are not interrupt-driven, the output of *sysdef* cannot be used for *config*. Because information regarding *config* aliases is not preserved by the system, device names returned might not be accurate.

NAME

  tic — terminfo compiler

SYNOPSIS

  tic [−v[*n*]] file ...

DESCRIPTION

  Tic translates terminfo files from the source format into the compiled format. The results are placed in the directory
  /usr/lib/terminfo.

  The −v (verbose) option causes *tic* to output trace information
  showing its progress. If the optional integer is appended, the level
  of verbosity can be increased.

  Tic compiles all terminfo descriptions in the given files. When a
  use= field is discovered, *tic* searches first the current file, then the
  master file, which is "./terminfo.src".

  If the environment variable TERMINFO is set, the results are
  placed there instead of **/usr/lib/terminfo**.

  Some limitations: total compiled entries cannot exceed 4096 bytes.
  The name field cannot exceed 128 bytes.

FILES

  /usr/lib/terminfo/*/*   compiled terminal capability data base

SEE ALSO

  curses(3X), terminfo(4) in the *UNIX Programmer's Manual —
  Volume 2: System Calls and Library Routines*.

BUGS

  Instead of searching **./terminfo.src**, it should check for an existing
  compiled entry.

NAME
   uuclean — uucp spool directory clean-up

SYNOPSIS
   /usr/lib/uucp/uuclean [options]

DESCRIPTION
   Uuclean will scan the spool directory for files with the specified
   prefix and delete all those which are older than the specified
   number of hours.

   The following options are available.

   −d*directory* Clean *directory* instead of the spool directory. If
   directory is not a valid spool directory it cannot contain "work files" i.e., files whose names start with
   "C.". These files have special meaning to **uuclean** per-
   taining to **uucp** job statistics.

   −p*pre* Scan for files with *pre* as the file prefix. Up to 10
   −**p** arguments may be specified. A −**p** without any
   pre following will cause all files older than the
   specified time to be deleted.

   −n*time* Files whose age is more than *time* hours will be
   deleted if the prefix test is satisfied. (default time is
   72 hours)

   −w*file* The default action for *uuclean* is to remove files
   which are older than a specified time (see −**n**
   option). The −**w** option is used to find those files
   older than *time* hours, however, the files are not
   deleted. If the argument *file* is present the warning
   is placed in *file*, otherwise, the warnings will go to
   the standard output.

   −s*sys* Only files destined for system *sys* are examined. Up
   to 10 −**s** arguments may be specified.

   −m*file* The −**m** option sends mail to the owner of the file
   when it is deleted. If a *file* is specified then an entry
   is placed in *file*.

   This program is typically started by *cron*(1M).

FILES

    /usr/lib/uucp   directory with commands used by *uuclean* internally

    /usr/spool/uucp   spool directory

SEE ALSO

    cron(1M).

    uucp(1C), uux(1C) in the *UNIX Programmer's Manual — Volume 1: Commands and Utilities*.

NAME

uusub — monitor uucp network

SYNOPSIS

/usr/lib/uucp/uusub [options]

DESCRIPTION

Uusub(1M) defines a *uucp* subnetwork and monitors the connection and traffic among the members of the subnetwork. The following options are available:

−a*sys*	Add *sys* to the subnetwork.
−d*sys*	Delete *sys* from the subnetwork.
−l	Report the statistics on connections.
−r	Report the statistics on traffic amount.
−f	Flush the connection statistics.
−u*hr*	Gather the traffic statistics over the past *hr* hours.
−c*sys*	Exercise the connection to the system *sys*. If *sys* is specified as **all**, then exercise the connection to all the systems in the subnetwork.

The meanings of the connections report are:

> sys #call #ok time #dev #login #nack #other

where *sys* is the remote system name, *#call* is the number of times the local system tries to call *sys* since the last flush was done, and *#ok* is the number of successful connections, *time* is the latest successful connect time, *#dev* is the number of unsuccessful connections because of no available device (e.g., ACU), *#login* is the number of unsuccessful connections because of login failure, *#nack* is the number of unsuccessful connections because of no response (e.g. line busy, system down), and *#other* is the number of unsuccessful connections because of other reasons.

The meanings of the traffic statistics are:

> sfile sbyte rfile rbyte

where *sfile* is the number of files sent and *sbyte* is the number of bytes sent over the period of time indicated in the latest *uusub* command with the −u*hr* option. Similarly, *rfile* and *rbyte* are the numbers of files and bytes received.

The command:

     uusub —c all —u 24

is typically started by *cron*(1M) once a day.

FILES

/usr/spool/uucp/SYSLOG	system log file
/usr/lib/uucp/L_sub	connection statistics
/usr/lib/uucp/R_sub	traffic statistics

SEE ALSO

uucp(1C), uustat(1C) in the *UNIX Programmer's Manual — Volume 1: Commands and Utilities.*

NAME
     volcopy, labelit — copy file systems with label checking

SYNOPSIS
     /etc/volcopy [options] fsname special1 volname1 special2 vol-
     name2

     /etc/labelit special [fsname volume [**−n**]]

DESCRIPTION
     Volcopy makes a literal copy of the file system using a blocksize
     matched to the device. *Options* are:
          −a   invoke a verification sequence requiring a positive
                  operator response instead of the standard 10-
                  second delay before the copy is made
          −s   (default) invoke the **DEL if wrong** verification
                  sequence.

     Other *options* are used only with tapes:
          −bpidensity   bits-per-inch (i.e., **800/1600/6250**),
          −feetsize   size of reel in feet (i.e., **1200/2400**),
          −reelnum   beginning reel number for a restarted copy,
          −buf   use double buffered I/O.

     The program requests length and density information if it is not
     given on the command line or is not recorded on an input tape
     label. If the file system is too large to fit on one reel, *volcopy* will
     prompt for additional reels. Labels of all reels are checked. Tapes
     may be mounted alternately on two or more drives. If *volcopy* is
     interrupted, it will ask if the user wants to quit or wants a shell.
     In the latter case, the user can perform other operations (e.g.,:
     labelit) and return to *volcopy* by exiting the new shell.

     The *fsname* argument represents the mounted name (e.g.,: **root**,
     u1, etc.) of the filsystem being copied.

     The *special* should be the physical disk section or tape (e.g.,:
     /dev/rdsk/1s5, /dev/rmt/0m, etc.).

     The *volname* is the physical volume name (e.g.,: **pk3, t0122**, etc.)
     and should match the external label sticker. Such label names are
     limited to six or fewer characters. *Volname* may be — to use the
     existing volume name.

     Special1 and *volname1* are the device and volume from which the
     copy of the file system is being extracted. *Special2* and *volname2*
     are the target device and volume.

Fsname and *volname* are recorded in the last 12 characters of the superblock (**char fsname[6], volname[6];**).

Labelit can be used to provide initial labels for unmounted disk or tape file systems. With the optional arguments omitted, *labelit* prints current label values. The **−n** option provides for initial labeling of new tapes only (this destroys previous contents).

FILES

/etc/log/filesave.log   a record of file systems/volumes copied

SEE ALSO

sh(1) in the *UNIX Programmer's Manual —Volume 1: Commands and Utilities*.
fs(4) in the *UNIX Programmer's Manual —Volume 2: System Calls and Library Routines*.

BUGS

Only device names beginning **/dev/rmt/** are treated as tapes.

NAME
      wall — write to all users

SYNOPSIS
      /etc/wall

DESCRIPTION
      Wall reads its standard input until an end-of-file. It then sends
      this message to all currently logged-in users preceded by:

            Broadcast Message from ...

      It is used to warn all users, typically prior to shutting down the
      system.

      The sender must be super-user to override any protections the
      users may have invoked (see *mesg*(1)).

FILES
      /dev/tty*

SEE ALSO
      mesg(1), write(1) in the *UNIX Programmer's Manual—Volume 1:
      Commands and Utilities.*

DIAGNOSTICS
      "Cannot send to ..." when the open on a user's tty file fails.

NAME
    whodo — who is doing what

SYNOPSIS
    /etc/whodo

DESCRIPTION
    Whodo produces merged, reformatted, and dated output from the
    who(1) and *ps*(1) commands.

FILES
    etc/passwd

SEE ALSO
    ps(1), who(1) in the *UNIX Programmer's Manual—Volume 1:*
    Commands and Utilities.

NAME

   intro — introduction to special files

DESCRIPTION

   This section describes various special files that refer to specific
   hardware peripherals and UNIX system device drivers. The names
   of the entries are generally derived from names for the hardware,
   as opposed to the names of the special files themselves. Characteristics of both the hardware device and the corresponding UNIX
   system device driver are discussed where applicable.

   Tape device file names are in the following format:

   /dev/{r}mt/(c#d)#[hml]{n}

   where **r** indicates a raw device, **c#d** indicates the controller
   number (which is optionally specified by the system administrator), **#** is the device number, **hml** indicates the density (**h** (high)
   for 6250 bpi, **m** (medium) for 1600 bpi, and **l** (low density) for
   800 bpi), and **n** indicates no rewind on close. (e.g., **/dev/mt/2mn**)

   Disk device file names are in the following format:

   /dev/{r}dsk/(r)(c#d)#s#

   where **r** indicates a raw interface to the disk, the second **r** indicates
   that this disk is on a remote system, the **c#d** indicates the controller number (which is optionally specified by the system
   administrator), and **#s#** indicates the drive and section numbers,
   respectively.

BUGS

   While the names of the entries *generally* refer to vendor hardware
   names, in certain cases these names are seemingly arbitrary for
   various historical reasons.

NAME

acu, dn — Automatic Call Unit (ACU) interface

DESCRIPTION

The ACU drivers support *close*(2), *open*(2), and *write*(2) system calls. In addition, the *tn8* driver on the 3B20 computer supports an *ioctl* system call. The **acu?** and **dn?** files are write-only. The *write* system call sends the telephone number to be dialed to the ACU. The permissible codes are:

0-9	dial 0-9
* or :	dial *
# or ;	dial #
—	4-second delay for second dial tone
e or <	end-of-number
w or =	wait for secondary dial tone
f	flash off hook for 1 second

The entire telephone number must be presented in a single *write* system call.

The *ioctl* system call (*tn8* only) is invoked as follows:

```
#include <sys/acu.h>
int fildes, cmd;
struct acutab *acutp;
ioctl (fildes, cmd, acutp);
```

Acutab is a table specifying the connections between ACU minor devices and communication lines:

```
struct acutab {
        int minor;
        int unit;
        int port;
        int line;
} acutab[NACU];
```

The *NACU* parameter is a constant from *acu.h* that specifies the number of lines the TN8 ACUs can dial out on.

The *ioctl cmds* are:

ACUSDEV—Specify a connection between an ACU minor device and a telephone line. This command makes an entry in *acutab*, the table that specifies associations between ACU minor devices and dial-out lines. Before the ACUs can be used, and after any ACU reconfiguration, this table must

be sent to the ACU peripheral controller via the ACUS-
TART command.

ACUSTART—Connect ACU minor devices to telephone lines. This
command informs the ACU peripheral controller of the
connections set up by the ACUSDEV command and
enables it.

SEE ALSO

close(2), ioctl(2), open(2), write(2) in the *UNIX Programmer's
Manual—Volume 2: System Calls and Library Routines.*

FILES

/dev/acu?	(3B20 computer only)
/dev/tn8	(3B20 computer only)
/dev/dn?	(DEC only)

NAME
    err — error-logging interface

DESCRIPTION
    Minor device 0 of the *err* driver is the interface between a process
    and the system's error-record collection routines. The driver may
    be opened only for reading by a single process with super-user per-
    missions. Each read causes an entire error record to be retrieved;
    the record is truncated if the read request is for less than the
    record's length.

FILES
    /dev/error   special file

SEE ALSO
    errdemon(1M).

NAME

mem, kmem — core memory

DESCRIPTION

Mem is a special file that is an image of the core memory of the computer. It may be used, for example, to examine, and even to patch the system.

Byte addresses in *mem* are interpreted as memory addresses. References to non-existent locations cause errors to be returned.

Examining and patching device registers is likely to lead to unexpected results when read-only or write-only bits are present.

The file *kmem* is the same as *mem* except that kernel virtual memory rather than physical memory is accessed.

On the PDP-11, the I/O page begins at location 0160000 of *kmem* and per-process data for the current process begins at 0140000.

FILES

/dev/mem
/dev/kmem

BUGS

On the PDP-11, memory files are accessed one byte at a time, an inappropriate method for some device registers.

NAME
   null — the null file

DESCRIPTION
   Data written on a null special file is discarded.

   Reads from a null special file always return 0 bytes.

FILES
   /dev/null

NAME
        prf — operating system profiler

DESCRIPTION
        The file **prf** provides access to activity information in the operating
        system. Writing the file loads the measurement facility with text
        addresses to be monitored. Reading the file returns these
        addresses and a set of counters indicative of activity between adja-
        cent text addresses.

        The recording mechanism is driven by the system clock and sam-
        ples the program counter at line frequency. Samples that catch
        the operating system are matched against the stored text addresses
        and increment corresponding counters for later processing.

        The file **prf** is a pseudo-device with no associated hardware.

FILES
        /dev/prf

SEE ALSO
        config(1M), profiler(1M).

NAME

    sxt — pseudo-device driver

DESCRIPTION

    Sxt is a pseudo-device driver that interposes a discipline between the standard *tty* line disciplines and a real device driver. The standard disciplines manipulate *virtual tty* structures (channels) declared by the *sxt* driver. *Sxt* acts as a discipline manipulating a *real tty* structure declared by a real device driver. The *sxt* driver is currently only used by the *shl* (1) command.

    Virtual ttys are named by inodes in the subdirectory **/dev/sxt** and are allocated in groups of up to eight. To allocate a group, a program should exclusively open a file with a name of the form **/dev/sxt/??0** (channel 0) and then execute a SXTIOCLINK *ioctl* call to initiate the multiplexing.

    Only one channel, the *controlling* channel, can receive input from the keyboard at a time; others attempting to read will be blocked.

    There are two groups of *ioctl* (2) commands supported by *sxt*. The first group contains the standard *ioctl* commands described in *termio* (7), with the addition of the following:

        TIOCEXCL   Set *exclusive use* mode: no further opens are permitted until the file has been closed.

        TIOCNXCL Reset *exclusive use* mode: further opens are once again permitted.

    The second group are directives to *sxt* itself. Some of these may only be executed on channel 0.

        SXTIOCLINK   Allocate a channel group and multiplex the virtual ttys onto the real tty. The argument is the number of channels to allocate. This command may only be executed on channel 0. Possible errors include:

                                          EINVAL   The argument is out of range.

                                          ENOTTY The command was not issued from a real tty.

ENXIO   *linesw* is not configured with *sxt*.

EBUSY   An SXTIOCLINK command has already been issued for this real *tty*.

ENOMEM

There is no system memory available for allocating the virtual tty structures.

EBADF   Channel 0 was not opened before this call.

SXTIOCSWTCH   Set the controlling channel. Possible errors include:

EINVAL   An invalid channel number was given.

EPERM   The command was not executed from channel 0.

SXTIOCWF   Cause a channel to wait until it is the controlling channel. This command will return the error, *EINVAL*, if an invalid channel number is given.

SXTIOCUBLK   Turn off the **loblk** control flag in the virtual tty of the indicated channel. The error *EINVAL* will be returned if an invalid number or channel 0 is given.

SXTIOCSTAT   Get the status (blocked on input or output) of each channel and store in the *sxtblock* structure referenced by the argument. The error *EFAULT* will be returned if the structure cannot be written.

SXTIOCTRACE   Enable tracing. Tracing information is written to */dev/osm* on the 3B20 computer or to the console on the VAX. This command has no effect if tracing is not configured.

SXTIOCNOTRACE Disable tracing. This command has
no effect if tracing is not configured.

FILES

/dev/sxt/??[0-7]   Virtual tty devices
/usr/include/sys/sxt.h   Driver specific definitions.

SEE ALSO

termio(7).

shl(1), stty(1) in the *UNIX Programmer's Manual—Volume 1:
Commands and Utilities*.

ioctl(2), open(2) in the *UNIX Programmer's Manual—Volume 2:
System Calls and Library Routines*.

NAME

　　termio — general terminal interface

DESCRIPTION

　　All of the asynchronous communications ports use the same general interface, no matter what hardware is involved. The remainder of this section discusses the common features of this interface.

　　When a terminal file is opened, it normally causes the process to wait until a connection is established. In practice, users' programs seldom open these files; they are opened by *getty* and become a user's standard input, output, and error files. The very first terminal file opened by the process group leader of a terminal file not already associated with a process group becomes the *control terminal* for that process group. The control terminal plays a special role in handling quit and interrupt signals, as discussed below. The control terminal is inherited by a child process during a *fork*(2). A process can break this association by changing its process group using *setpgrp*(2).

　　A terminal associated with one of these files ordinarily operates in full-duplex mode. Characters may be typed at any time, even while output is occurring, and are only lost when the system's character input buffers become completely full, which is rare, or when the user has accumulated the maximum allowed number of input characters that have not yet been read by some program. Currently, this limit is 256 characters. When the input limit is reached, all the saved characters are thrown away without notice.

　　Normally, terminal input is processed in units of lines. A line is delimited by a new-line (ASCII LF) character, an end-of-file (ASCII EOT) character, or an end-of-line character. This means that a program attempting to read will be suspended until an entire line has been typed. Also, no matter how many characters are requested in the read call, at most one line will be returned. It is not, however, necessary to read a whole line at once; any number of characters may be requested in a read, even one, without losing information.

　　During input, erase and kill processing is normally done. By default, the character # erases the last character typed, except that it will not erase beyond the beginning of the line. By default, the character @ kills (deletes) the entire input line, and optionally outputs a new-line character. Both these characters operate on a key-stroke basis, independently of any backspacing or tabbing that may have been done. Both the erase and kill characters may be entered literally by preceding them with the escape character (\). In this case the escape character is not read. The erase and kill characters may be changed.

Certain characters have special functions on input. These functions and their default character values are summarized as follows:

INTR   (Rubout or ASCII DEL) generates an *interrupt* signal which is sent to all processes with the associated control terminal. Normally, each such process is forced to terminate, but arrangements may be made either to ignore the signal or to receive a trap to an agreed-upon location; see *signal*(2).

QUIT   (Control-| or ASCII FS) generates a *quit* signal. Its treatment is identical to the interrupt signal except that, unless a receiving process has made other arrangements, it will not only be terminated but a core image file (called **core**) will be created in the current working directory.

SWTCH   (Control-z or ASCII SUB) is used by the job control facility, *shl,* to change the current layer to the control layer.

ERASE   (#) erases the preceding character. It will not erase beyond the start of a line, as delimited by a NL, EOF, or EOL character.

KILL   (@) deletes the entire line, as delimited by a NL, EOF, or EOL character.

EOF   (Control-d or ASCII EOT) may be used to generate an end-of-file from a terminal. When received, all the characters waiting to be read are immediately passed to the program, without waiting for a new-line, and the EOF is discarded. Thus, if there are no characters waiting, which is to say the EOF occurred at the beginning of a line, zero characters will be passed back, which is the standard end-of-file indication.

NL   (ASCII LF) is the normal line delimiter. It can not be changed or escaped.

EOL   (ASCII NUL) is an additional line delimiter, like NL. It is not normally used.

STOP   (Control-s or ASCII DC3) can be used to temporarily suspend output. It is useful with CRT terminals to prevent output from disappearing before it can be read. While output is suspended, STOP characters are ignored and not read.

START   (Control-q or ASCII DC1) is used to resume output which has been suspended by a STOP character. While output is not suspended, START characters are ignored and not read. The start/stop characters can not be changed or escaped.

The character values for INTR, QUIT, SWTCH, ERASE, KILL, EOF, and EOL may be changed to suit individual tastes. The ERASE, KILL, and EOF characters may be escaped by a preceding \ character, in which case no special function is done.

When the carrier signal from the data-set drops, a *hang-up* signal is sent to all processes that have this terminal as the control terminal. Unless other arrangements have been made, this signal causes the processes to terminate. If the hang-up signal is ignored, any subsequent read returns with an end-of-file indication. Thus, programs that read a terminal and test for end-of-file can terminate appropriately when hung up on.

When one or more characters are written, they are transmitted to the terminal as soon as previously-written characters have finished typing. Input characters are echoed by putting them in the output queue as they arrive. If a process produces characters more rapidly than they can be typed, it will be suspended when its output queue exceeds some limit. When the queue has drained down to some threshold, the program is resumed.

Several *ioctl* (2) system calls apply to terminal files. The primary calls use the following structure, defined in **<termio.h>**:

```
#define   NCC      8
struct    termio {
          unsigned   short   c_iflag;      /* input modes */
          unsigned   short   c_oflag;      /* output modes */
          unsigned   short   c_cflag;      /* control modes */
          unsigned   short   c_lflag;      /* local modes */
          char               c_line;       /* line discipline */
          unsigned   char    c_cc[NCC];    /* control chars */
};
```

The special control characters are defined by the array c_cc. The relative positions and initial values for each function are as follows:

0	VINTR	DEL
1	VQUIT	FS
2	VERASE	#
3	VKILL	@
4	VEOF	EOT
5	VEOL	NUL
6	reserved	
7	SWTCH	

The c_iflag field describes the basic terminal input control:

IGNBRK	0000001	Ignore break condition.
BRKINT	0000002	Signal interrupt on break.
IGNPAR	0000004	Ignore characters with parity errors.
PARMRK	0000010	Mark parity errors.
INPCK	0000020	Enable input parity check.
ISTRIP	0000040	Strip character.
INLCR	0000100	Map NL to CR on input.
IGNCR	0000200	Ignore CR.
ICRNL	0000400	Map CR to NL on input.
IUCLC	0001000	Map upper-case to lower-case on input.
IXON	0002000	Enable start/stop output control.
IXANY	0004000	Enable any character to restart output.
IXOFF	0010000	Enable start/stop input control.

If IGNBRK is set, the break condition (a character framing error with data all zeros) is ignored, that is, not put on the input queue and therefore not read by any process. Otherwise if BRKINT is set, the break condition will generate an interrupt signal and flush both the input and output queues. If IGNPAR is set, characters with other framing and parity errors are ignored.

If PARMRK is set, a character with a framing or parity error which is not ignored is read as the three-character sequence: 0377, 0, X, where X is the data of the character received in error. To avoid ambiguity in this case, if ISTRIP is not set, a valid character of 0377 is read as 0377, 0377. If PARMRK is not set, a framing or parity error which is not ignored is read as the character NUL (0).

If INPCK is set, input parity checking is enabled. If INPCK is not set, input parity checking is disabled. This allows output parity generation without input parity errors.

If ISTRIP is set, valid input characters are first stripped to 7-bits, otherwise all 8-bits are processed.

If INLCR is set, a received NL character is translated into a CR character. If IGNCR is set, a received CR character is ignored (not read). Otherwise if ICRNL is set, a received CR character is translated into a NL character.

If IUCLC is set, a received upper-case alphabetic characters translated into the corresponding lower-case character.

If IXON is set, start/stop output control is enabled. A received STOP character will suspend output and a received START character will restart output. All start/stop characters are ignored and not read. If IXANY is set, any input character, will restart output which has been suspended.

If IXOFF is set, the system will transmit START/STOP characters when the input queue is nearly empty/full.

The initial input control value is all-bits-clear.

The *c_oflag* field specifies the system treatment of output:

OPOST	0000001	Postprocess output.
OLCUC	0000002	Map lower case to upper on output.
ONLCR	0000004	Map NL to CR-NL on output.
OCRNL	0000010	Map CR to NL on output.
ONOCR	0000020	No CR output at column 0.
ONLRET	0000040	NL performs CR function.
OFILL	0000100	Use fill characters for delay.
OFDEL	0000200	Fill is DEL, else NUL.
NLDLY	0000400	Select new-line delays:
NL0	0	
NL1	0000400	
CRDLY	0003000	Select carriage-return delays:
CR0	0	
CR1	0001000	
CR2	0002000	
CR3	0003000	
TABDLY	0014000	Select horizontal-tab delays:
TAB0	0	
TAB1	0004000	
TAB2	0010000	
TAB3	0014000	Expand tabs to spaces.
BSDLY	0020000	Select backspace delays:

BS0	0	
BS1	0020000	
VTDLY	0040000	Select vertical-tab delays:
VT0	0	
VT1	0040000	
FFDLY	0100000	Select form-feed delays:
FF0	0	
FF1	0100000	

If OPOST is set, output characters are post-processed as indicated by the remaining flags, otherwise characters are transmitted without change.

If OLCUC is set, a lower-case alphabetic character is transmitted as the corresponding upper-case character. This function is often used in conjunction with IUCLC.

If ONLCR is set, the NL character is transmitted as the CR-NL character pair. If OCRNL is set, the CR character is transmitted as the NL character. If ONOCR is set, no CR character is transmitted when at column 0 (first position). If ONLRET is set, the NL character is assumed to do the carriage-return function; the column pointer will be set to 0 and the delays specified for CR will be used. Otherwise the NL character is assumed to do just the line-feed function; the column pointer will remain unchanged. The column pointer is also set to 0 if the CR character is actually transmitted.

The delay bits specify how long transmission stops to allow for mechanical or other movement when certain characters are sent to the terminal. In all cases a value of 0 indicates no delay. If OFILL is set, fill characters will be transmitted for delay instead of a timed delay. This is useful for high baud rate terminals which need only a minimal delay. If OFDEL is set, the fill character is DEL, otherwise NUL.

If a form-feed or vertical-tab delay is specified, it lasts for about 2 seconds.

New-line delay lasts about 0.10 seconds. If ONLRET is set, the carriage-return delays are used instead of the new-line delays. If OFILL is set, two fill characters will be transmitted.

Carriage-return delay type 1 is dependent on the current column position, type 2 is about 0.10 seconds, and type 3 is about 0.15 seconds. If OFILL is set, delay type 1 transmits two fill characters, and type 2, four fill characters.

Horizontal-tab delay type 1 is dependent on the current column position. Type 2 is about 0.10 seconds. Type 3 specifies that tabs are to be expanded into spaces. If OFILL is set, two fill characters will be transmitted for any delay.

Backspace delay lasts about 0.05 seconds. If OFILL is set, one fill character will be transmitted.

The actual delays depend on line speed and system load.

The initial output control value is all bits clear.

The *c_cflag* field describes the hardware control of the terminal:

CBAUD	0000017	Baud rate:
B0	0	Hang up
B50	0000001	50 baud
B75	0000002	75 baud
B110	0000003	110 baud
B134	0000004	134.5 baud
B150	0000005	150 baud
B200	0000006	200 baud
B300	0000007	300 baud
B600	0000010	600 baud
B1200	0000011	1200 baud
B1800	0000012	1800 baud
B2400	0000013	2400 baud
B4800	0000014	4800 baud
B9600	0000015	9600 baud
EXTA	0000016	External A
EXTB	0000017	External B
CSIZE	0000060	Character size:
CS5	0	5 bits
CS6	0000020	6 bits
CS7	0000040	7 bits
CS8	0000060	8 bits
CSTOPB	0000100	Send two stop bits, else one.
CREAD	0000200	Enable receiver.
PARENB	0000400	Parity enable.
PARODD	0001000	Odd parity, else even.
HUPCL	0002000	Hang up on last close.

CLOCAL	0004000	Local line, else dial-up.
LOBLK	0010000	Block layer output.

The CBAUD bits specify the baud rate. The zero baud rate, B0, is used to hang up the connection. If B0 is specified, the data-terminal-ready signal will not be asserted. Normally, this will disconnect the line. For any particular hardware, impossible speed changes are ignored.

The CSIZE bits specify the character size in bits for both transmission and reception. This size does not include the parity bit, if any. If CSTOPB is set, two stop bits are used, otherwise one stop bit. For example, at 110 baud, two stops bits are required.

If PARENB is set, parity generation and detection is enabled and a parity bit is added to each character. If parity is enabled, the PARODD flag specifies odd parity if set, otherwise even parity is used.

If CREAD is set, the receiver is enabled. Otherwise no characters will be received.

If HUPCL is set, the line will be disconnected when the last process with the line open closes it or terminates. That is, the data-terminal-ready signal will not be asserted.

If CLOCAL is set, the line is assumed to be a local, direct connection with no modem control. Otherwise modem control is assumed.

If LOBLK is set, the output of a job control layer will be blocked when it is not the current layer. Otherwise the output generated by that layer will be multiplexed onto the current layer.

The initial hardware control value after open is B300, CS8, CREAD, HUPCL.

The *c_lflag* field of the argument structure is used by the line discipline to control terminal functions. The basic line discipline (0) provides the following:

ISIG	0000001	Enable signals.
ICANON	0000002	Canonical input (erase and kill processing).
XCASE	0000004	Canonical upper/lower presentation.
ECHO	0000010	Enable echo.
ECHOE	0000020	Echo erase character as BS-SP-BS.
ECHOK	0000040	Echo NL after kill character.
ECHONL	0000100	Echo NL.

NOFLSH   0000200 Disable flush after interrupt or quit.

If ISIG is set, each input character is checked against the special control characters INTR, SWTCH, and QUIT. If an input character matches one of these control characters, the function associated with that character is performed. If ISIG is not set, no checking is done. Thus these special input functions are possible only if ISIG is set. These functions may be disabled individually by changing the value of the control character to an unlikely or impossible value (e.g., 0377).

If ICANON is set, canonical processing is enabled. This enables the erase and kill edit functions, and the assembly of input characters into lines delimited by NL, EOF, and EOL. If ICANON is not set, read requests are satisfied directly from the input queue. A read will not be satisfied until at least MIN characters have been received or the timeout value TIME has expired between characters. This allows fast bursts of input to be read efficiently while still allowing single character input. The MIN and TIME values are stored in the position for the EOF and EOL characters, respectively. The time value represents tenths of seconds.

If XCASE is set, and if ICANON is set, an upper-case letter is accepted on input by preceding it with a \ character, and is output preceded by a \ character. In this mode, the following escape sequences are generated on output and accepted on input:

for:	*use*:
`	\\'
|	\\!
	\\^
{	\\(
}	\\)
\\	\\\\

For example, A is input as \a, \n as \\n, and \N as \\\n.

If ECHO is set, characters are echoed as received.

When ICANON is set, the following echo functions are possible. If ECHO and ECHOE are set, the erase character is echoed as ASCII BS SP BS, which will clear the last character from a CRT screen. If ECHOE is set and ECHO is not set, the erase character is echoed as ASCII SP BS. If ECHOK is set, the NL character will be echoed after the kill character to emphasize that the line will be deleted. Note that an escape character preceding the erase or kill character removes any special function. If ECHONL is set, the NL character will be echoed even if ECHO is not set. This is useful for terminals set to local echo (so-called half duplex). Unless escaped, the EOF character is not echoed. Because EOT is the default EOF character, this prevents terminals that respond to EOT from hanging up.

If NOFLSH is set, the normal flush of the input and output queues associated with the quit, switch, and interrupt characters will not be done.

The initial line-discipline control value is all bits clear.

The primary *ioctl* (2) system calls have the form:

    ioctl (fildes, command, arg)
    struct termio *arg;

The commands using this form are:

TCGETA   Get the parameters associated with the terminal and store in the *termio* structure referenced by **arg**.

TCSETA   Set the parameters associated with the terminal from the structure referenced by **arg**. The change is immediate.

TCSETAW   Wait for the output to drain before setting the new parameters. This form should be used when changing parameters that will affect output.

TCSETAF   Wait for the output to drain, then flush the input queue and set the new parameters.

Additional *ioctl* (2) calls have the form:

    ioctl (fildes, command, arg)
    int arg;

The commands using this form are:

TCSBRK   Wait for the output to drain. If *arg* is 0, then send a break (zero bits for 0.25 seconds).

TCXONC   Start/stop control. If *arg* is 0, suspend output; if 1, restart suspended output.

TCFLSH   If *arg* is 0, flush the input queue; if 1, flush
              the output queue; if 2, flush both the input
              and output queues.

FILES

/dev/tty*

SEE ALSO

stty(1) in the *UNIX Programmer's Manual—Volume 1: Commands and Utilities.*
fork(2), ioctl(2), setpgrp(2), signal(2) in the *UNIX Programmer's Manual—Volume 2: System Calls and Library Routines.*

NAME

 trace — event-tracing driver

DESCRIPTION

 Trace is a special file that allows event records generated within the UNIX system kernel to be passed to a user program so that the activity of a driver or other system routines can be monitored for debugging purposes.

 An event record is generated from within a kernel driver or system routine by invoking the *trsave* function:

 trsave (dev, chno, buf, cnt)
 char   dev, chno, *buf, cnt;

 Dev is a minor device number of the trace driver; *chno* is an integer between 0 and 15 inclusive that identifies the data stream (channel) to which the record belongs; *buf* is a buffer containing the data for an event; and *cnt* is the number of bytes in *buf*. Calls to *trsave* will result in data being placed on a queue, provided that some user program has opened the trace minor device *dev* and has enabled channel *chno*. Event records consisting of a time stamp (4 bytes), the channel number (1 byte), the count (1 byte), and the event data (*cnt* bytes) are stored on a queue until a system-defined maximum (TRQMAX) is reached; an event record is discarded if there is not sufficient room on the queue for the entire record. The queue is emptied by a user program reading the trace driver. Each *read* returns an integral number of event records; the read count must, therefore, be at least equal to *cnt* plus six.

 The *trace* driver supports *open, close(2), ioctl(2),* and *read(2),* system calls. The *ioctl* system call is invoked as follows:

 #include <sys/vpm.h>
 int fildes, cmd, arg;
 ioctl (fildes, cmd, arg);

 The values for the *cmd* argument are:

 VPMSETC—Enable trace channels. This command enables each channel indicated by a 1 in the bit mask found in *arg*. The low-order bit (bit 0) corresponds to channel zero, the next bit (bit 1) corresponds to channel 1, etc.

 VPMGETC—Get enabled channels. This command returns in *arg* a bit mask containing a 1 for each channel that is currently enabled.

VPMCLRC—Disable channels. This command disables the channels indicated by a 1 in the bit mask found in *arg*.

SEE ALSO

close(2), ioctl(2), open(2), read(2) in the *UNIX Programmer's
Manual—Volume 2: System Calls and Library Routines.*

NAME

tty − controlling terminal interface

DESCRIPTION

The file **/dev/tty** is, in each process, a synonym for the control terminal associated with the process group of that process, if any. It
is useful for programs or shell sequences that wish to be sure of
writing messages on the terminal no matter how output has been
redirected. It can also be used for programs that demand the
name of a file for output, when typed output is desired and it is
tiresome to find out what terminal is currently in use.

FILES

/dev/tty
/dev/tty*

NAME

intro — introduction to system maintenance procedures

DESCRIPTION

This section outlines certain procedures that will be of interest to those charged with the task of system maintenance.

NAME

   mk — how to remake the system and commands

DESCRIPTION

   All source for the UNIX system is in a source tree distributed in
   the directory **/usr/src**. This includes source for the operating system, libraries, commands, miscellaneous files necessary to the running system, and procedures to create everything from this source.

   The top level consists of the directories **cmd, lib, uts, head,** and
   stand as well as commands to remake each of these "directories".
   These commands are named *:mk*, which remakes everything, and
   :mk **dir** where **dir** is the directory to be recreated. Each recreation
   command will make all or part of the piece, over which it has control. The command *:mk* will run each of these commands and
   thus recreate the whole system.

   The **lib** directory contains libraries used when loading user programs. The largest and most important of these is the C library.
   All libraries are in sub-directories and are created by a makefile or
   runcom. A runcom is a shell command procedure used specifically
   to remake a piece of the system. *:mklib* will rebuild the libraries
   that are given as arguments. The argument * will cause it to
   remake all libraries.

   The **head** directory contains the header files, usually found in
   /usr/include on the running system. *:mkhead* will install those
   header files that are given as arguments. The argument * will
   cause it to install all header files.

   The **uts** directory contains the source for the UNIX operating system. *:mkuts* (no arguments) invokes a series of makefiles that will
   recreate the operating system.

   The **stand** directory contains stand-alone commands and boot programs. *:mkstand* will rebuild and install these programs.

   The **cmd** directory contains files and directories. *:mkcmd*
   transforms source into a command based upon its suffix (**.l, .y, .c,
   .s, .sh**), or its makefile (see *make*(1)) or runcom. A directory is
   assumed to have a makefile or a runcom that will take care of
   creating everything associated with that directory and its sub-
   directories. Makefiles and runcoms are named *command*.**mk** and
   command.**rc** respectively.

   The command *:mkcmd* will recreate commands based upon a
   makefile or runcom if one of them exists; alternatively commands

rjerecv   Cycles repetitively, looking for data returning from the
IBM machine. Upon receipt of data, *rjerecv* notifies either
rjexmit or *rjedisp* of the event (transfer information is
sometimes passed to *rjexmit*). *Rjerecv* exits normally at
the first appropriate moment when it encounters the file
stop, or exits reluctantly when it encounters a run of
errors.

rjedisp   Follows up event notices by directing output files, updating
records, and notifying users. *Rjedisp* references the system files **/etc/passwd** and **/etc/utmp** to correlate user
names, numeric ids, and terminals. Termination of
rjerecv causes *rjedisp* to exit also.

Rjeinit has the capability of *dialing* any remote IBM system with
the proper hardware and software configuration.

Most RJE files and directories are protected from unauthorized
tampering. The exception is the **spool** directory. It is used by
send (1C) to create temporary files in the correct file system.
Rjeqer and *rjestat* (1C), the user's interfaces to RJE, operate in
setuid mode to contribute the necessary permission modes.

Administration

Some minimal oversight of each RJE subsystem is required. The
RJE mailbox should be inspected and cleaned out periodically.
The **job** directory should also be checked. The only files placed
there are output files whose destination file systems are out of
space. Users should be given a short period of time (say, a day or
two), and then these files should be removed.

The configuration table **/usr/rje/lines** is accessed by all com-
ponents of RJE. Each line of the table (maximum of 8) defines an
RJE connection. Its seven columns may be labeled *host*, *system*,
directory, *prefix*, *device*, *peripherals* and *parameters*. These
columns are described as follows:

host

The name of a remote IBM computer (e.g., **A B C**). This
string can be up to 5 characters.

system

The nodename of a UNIX system. This name should be
the same as the nodename from *uname* (1).

directory
> This is the directory name of the servicing RJE subsystem (e.g., **/usr/rje1**).

prefix
> This is the string prefixed (redundantly) to several crucial files and programs in **directory** (e.g., **rje1, rje2, rje3**).

device
> This is the name of the controlling VPM device, with **/dev/** excised.

peripherals
> This field contains information on the logical devices (readers, printers, punches) used by RJE. Each subfield is separated by :, and is described as follows:
>
> (1) Number of logical readers.
> (2) Number of logical printers.
> (3) Number of logical punches.
>
> Note: the number of peripherals specified for an RJE subsystem **must** agree with the number of peripherals which have been described on the remote machine for that line.

parameters
> This field contains information on the type of connection to make. Each subfield is separated by :. Any or all fields may be omitted; however, the fields are positional. All but trailing delimiters must be present. For example, in
> $$1200:512:::9-555-1212$$
> subfields 3 and 4 are missing, but the delimiters are present. Each subfield is defined as follows:
>
> (1) **space**
>> This subfield specifies the amount of space (S) in blocks that RJE tries to maintain on file systems it touches. The default is 0 blocks. *Send* will not submit jobs, and *rjeinit* issues a warning when less than $1.5S$ blocks are available; *rjerecv* stops accepting output from the host when the capacity falls to S blocks; RJE becomes dormant, until conditions improve. If the space on the file system specified by the user on the "usr=" card would be depleted to a point below S, the file will be put in

the **job** subdirectory of the connection's home directory, rather than in the place that the user requested.

(2) **size**

This subfield specifies the size in blocks of the largest file that can be accepted from the host without truncation taking place. The default is no truncation.

(3) **badjobs**

This subfield specifies what to do with undeliverable returning jobs. If an output file is undeliverable for any reason other than file system space limitations (e.g., missing or invalid "usr=" card) and this subfield contains the letter **y**, the output will be retained in the **job** subdirectory of the home directory, and login **rje** is notified. If this subfield contains an **n** or has any other value, undeliverable output will be discarded. The default is **n**.

(4) **console**

This subfield specifies the status of the interactive status terminal for this line. If the subfield contains an **i**, all console status facilities are inhibited (e.g., *rjestat* (1C) will not behave like a status terminal). In all cases, the normal non-interactive uses of *rjestat* (1C) will continue to function. The default is **y**.

(5) **dial-up**

This subfield contains a telephone number to be used to call a host machine. The telephone number may contain the digits 0 through 9 and the character − which denotes a pause. If the telephone number is not present, no dialing is attempted and a leased line is assumed.

(6) **transmission block size**

This subfield specifies the size (in bytes) of transmission blocks to be sent to the IBM host for a particular rje subsystem. The maximum permitted block size is 512. The default is 512.

Sign-on is controlled by the existence of a **signon** file in the home directory. If this file is present, its contents are sent as a sign-on message to the host system. If this file does not exist, a blank card is sent. Sign-off is controlled in the same way, except that the **signoff** file is sent by *rjehalt* if it exists. If the **signoff** file does not exist, a "**/*signoff**" card is sent. These files should be ASCII text and no more than 80 characters.

Send(1C) and *rjestat*(1C) select an available connection by indexing on the **host** field of the configuration table. RJE programs index on the **prefix** field. A subordinate directory, **sque**, exists in **/usr/rje** for use by *rjedisp* and *shqer* programs. This directory holds those output files that have been designated as standard input to some executable file. This designation is done via the "usr=..." specification. *Rjedisp* places the output files here and updates the file **log** to specify the order of execution, arguments to be passed, etc. *Shqer* executes the appropriate files.

All RJE programs are shared text; therefore, if more than one RJE is to be run on a given UNIX system, simply link (via *ln*) RJE2 program names to RJE names in **/usr**.

SEE ALSO
mk(8).
cp(1), rjestat(1C), send(1C), uname(1) in the *UNIX Programmer's Manual Volume 1: Commands and Utilities.*
pnch(4) in the *UNIX Programmer's Manual Volume 2: System Calls and Library Routines.*

DIAGNOSTICS
Rjeinit provides brief error messages describing obstacles encountered while bringing up RJE. They can best be understood in the context of the RJE source code. The most frequently occurring one is "cannot open /dev/vpm?". This may occur if the VPM script has not been started, or if another process already has the VPM device open.

Once RJE has been started, users should assist in monitoring its performance, and should notify operations personnel of any perceived need for remedial action. *Rjestat*(1C) will aid in diagnosing the current state of RJE. It can detect, with some reliability, when the far end of the communications line has gone dead, and will report in this case that the host computer is not responding to RJE.

NAME

rje − RJE (Remote Job Entry) to IBM

SYNOPSIS

/usr/rje/rjeinit
/usr/rje/rjehalt

DESCRIPTION

RJE is the communal name for a collection of programs and a file
organization that allows a UNIX system, equipped with the
appropriate hardware and associated Virtual Protocol Machine
(VPM) software, to communicate with IBM's Job Entry Subsystems by mimicking an IBM 360 remote work station.

Implementation.

RJE is initiated by the command *rjeinit* and is terminated grace-
fully by the command *rjehalt*. While active, RJE runs in the
background and requires no human supervision. It quietly
transmits, to the IBM system, jobs that have been queued by the
send (1C) command, and operator requests that have been entered
by the *rjestat* (1C) command. It receives, from the IBM system,
print and punch data sets and message output. It enters the data
sets into the proper UNIX system directory and notifies the
appropriate user of their arrival. It stores the message output in
the file **resp** and makes these messages available for public inspec-
tion, so that *rjestat* (1C), in particular, may extract responses.

Unless otherwise specified, all files and commands described below
reside in directory **/usr/rje** (first exceptions: *send* and *rjestat*).

There are two sources of data to be transmitted by RJE from the
UNIX system to an IBM System/370. In both cases, the data is
organized as files in the **/usr/rje/squeue** directory. The first are
files named **co** which are created by the enquiry command
rjestat (1C). The second source, containing the bulk of the data,
are files named **rd** or **sq** which have been created by *send* (1C)
and queued by the program *rjeqer*. On completion of processing
send invokes *rjeqer*. *Rjeqer* and *rjestat1C* inform the program
rjexmit that a file has been queued via the file **joblog**. Upon successful transmission of the data to the IBM machine, *rjexmit*
removes the queued file. As files are transmitted and received, the
program *rjedisp* writes an entry containing the date, time, file
name, logname, and number of records in the file **acctlog**, if it
exists. This file can be used for local logging or accounting information, but is not used elsewhere by RJE. The use of this

information is up to the RJE administrator.

Each time *rjeinit* is invoked, the **joblog** file is truncated and recreated from the contents of the **/usr/rje/squeue** directory. During this time, *rjeinit* prevents simultaneous updating of the **joblog** file.

Output from the IBM system is classified as either a print data set, a punch data set, or message output. Print output is converted to an ASCII text file with standard tabs. Form feeds are suppressed, but the last line of each page is distinguished by the presence of an extraneous trailing space. Punch output is converted to *pnch*(4) format. This classification and both conversions occur as the output is received. Files are moved or copied into the appropriate user's directory and assigned the name **prnt*** or **pnch***, respectively, or placed into user directories under user-specified names, or used as input to programs to be automatically executed, as specified by the user. This process is driven by the "usr=..." specification. RJE retains ownership of these files and permits read-only access to them. Message output is digested by RJE immediately and is not retained.

A record is maintained for each job that passes through RJE. Identifying information is extracted contextually from files transmitted to and received from the IBM system.

Status messages are returned from IBM in response to enquiries entered by users. All messages received by RJE are appended to the **resp** file. The **resp** file is automatically truncated when it reaches 70,000 bytes. Each enquiry is preceded and followed by an identification card image of the form "$UX<*process id*>". The IBM system will echo this back as an illegal command. The appearance of process ids in the response stream permits responses to be passed on to the proper users.

While it is active, RJE occupies at least the three process slots that are appropriated by *rjeinit*. These slots are used to run *rjexmit*, the transmitter, *rjerecv*, the receiver, and *rjedisp*, the dispatcher. These three processes are connected by pipes. The function of each is as follows:

rjexmit Cycles repetitively, looking for data to transmit to the IBM system. After transmission, *rjexmit* passes an event notice to *rjedisp*. If *rjexmit* encounters a **stop** file, (created by *rjehalt*), it exits normally. In the case of error termination, *rjexmit* reboots RJE by executing *rjeinit*.

are recreated in a standard way based on the suffix of the source file. All commands requiring more than one file of source are grouped in sub-directories, and must have a makefile or a runcom. C programs (.c) are compiled by the C compiler and loaded stripped with shared text. Assembly language programs (.s) are assembled with **/usr/include/sys.s** which contains the system call definitions. Yacc programs (.y) and lex programs (.l) are processed by *yacc*(1) and *lex*(1) respectively, before C compilation. Shell programs (.sh) are copied to create the command. Each of these operations leaves a command in **./cmd** which is then installed by using **/etc/install**.

The arguments to *:mkcmd* are either command names or subsystem names. The subsystems distributed with the UNIX system are: **acct, graf, rje, sccs,** and **text**. Prefacing the *:mkcmd* instruction with an assignment to the shell variable **$ARGS** will cause the indicated components of the subsystem to be rebuilt. The entire **sccs** subsystem can be rebuilt by:

> /usr/src/:mkcmd sccs

while the *delta* component of **sccs** can be rebuilt by:

> ARGS="delta" /usr/src/:mkcmd sccs

The *log* command, which is a part of the **stat** package, which is itself a part of the **graf** package, can be rebuilt by:

> ARGS="stat log" /usr/src/:mkcmd graf

The argument * will cause all commands and subsystems to be rebuilt.

Makefiles, both in **./cmd** and in sub-directories, have a standard format. In particular *:mkcmd* depends on there being entries for *install* and *clobber*. *Install* should cause everything over which the makefile has jurisdiction to be made and installed by **/etc/install**. *Clobber* should cause a complete cleanup of all unnecessary files resulting from the previous invocation.

Most of the runcoms in **./cmd** (as opposed to sub-directories) relate in particular to a need for separated instruction and data (I and D) space.

In the past, dependency on the C library routine *ctime*(3C) was also important. *Ctime* had to be modified for all systems located outside of the eastern time zone, and all commands that referenced it had to be recompiled. *Ctime* has been rewritten to check the environment (see *environ*(5)) for the time zone. This results in time zone conversions possible on a per-process basis. The file **/etc/profile** sets the initial environment for each user, and **/etc/rc** sets it for certain system daemons. These two programs are the only ones which must be modified outside of the eastern time zone.

An effort has been made to separate the creation of a command from source, and its installation on the running system. The command **/etc/install** is used by *:mkcmd* and most makefiles to install commands in the proper place on the running system. The use of install allows maximum flexibility in the administration of the system. Install makes very few assumptions about where a command is located, who owns it, and what modes are in effect. All assumptions may be overridden on invocation of the command, or more permanently by redefining a few variables in install. The object is to install a new version of a command in the same place, with the same attributes as the prior version.

In addition, the use of a separate command to perform installation allows for the creation of test systems in other than standard places, easy movement of commands to balance load, and independent maintenance of makefiles. The minimization of makefiles in most cases, and the site independence of the others should greatly reduce the necessary maintenance, and allow makefiles to be considered part of the standard source.

SEE ALSO

install(1M).

lex(1), make(1), yacc(1) in the *UNIX Programmer's Manual — Volume 1: Commands and Utilities.*

ctime(3C), environ(5) in the *UNIX Programmer's Manual — Volume 2: System Calls and Library Routines.*